University of St. Francis
GEN   428 W733 2 ed.
Willis, Hulon.
A brief handbook of English /

3 0301 00074273 0

S0-AYE-929

A Brief
Handbook
of English

Second Edition

A Brief Handbook of English

Second Edition

Hulon Willis
Late of Bakersfield College

Enno Klammer
Eastern Oregon State College

LIBRARY
College of St. Francis
JOLIET, ILLINOIS

Harcourt Brace Jovanovich, Publishers
San Diego/New York/Chicago/Washington, D.C./Atlanta
London/Sydney/Toronto

Copyright © 1981, 1975 by Harcourt Brace Jovanovich, Inc.

All rights reserved. No part of this publication may be
reproduced or transmitted in any form or by any means,
electronic or mechanical, including photocopy, recording,
or any information storage and retrieval system,
without permission in writing from the publisher.

Requests for permission to make copies of any part
of the work should be mailed to: Permissions,
Harcourt Brace Jovanovich, Inc., 757 Third Avenue,
New York, N.Y. 10017.

ISBN: 0-15-505556-9

Library of Congress Catalog Card Number: 80-85075

Printed in the United States of America

428
W733
2ed

Preface

This second edition of *A Brief Handbook of English* retains the compact format of the original. Instructors familiar with the book through its first edition will find an old friend. Those who are new to it will readily note that it is designed to help students improve the conciseness, clarity, and correctness of their writing. An *Exercise Book* to accompany *A Brief Handbook of English* provides exercises or tests, so that an instructor may use the handbook as a teaching text as well as a reference work.

Changes in content respond to changing needs. Chapter 17, "The Research Paper," now conforms to the *MLA Handbook* (1977). Additional changes include revision of the definition of the sentence, a more forthright discussion of subject-verb agreement, an expanded treatment of the subjunctive, and a clarification of essential and nonessential constituents. New illustrations and examples have been introduced throughout.

One of the primary assumptions of this book is that the average student cannot, in one term, master the basics

,145,000

as well as the refinements of writing. For that reason, this second edition again avoids such subtleties of grammar as "squinting modifiers" and such disputed areas of usage as "reason is because." The book does not bog down in lists of exceptions. Short explanations are presented—rather than exhaustive analyses—of why the rules are what they are. Students learn in a straightforward manner what they may safely and correctly use. In that sense some may call it prescriptive; as a handbook of grammar and usage, it takes a positive stance in presenting basic rules that students can rely on.

In so far as possible, each section of the book is self-contained and offers a minimum of technical explanation. Since students using the book in a nonsequential way may encounter unfamiliar terms that are not explained at that point, the opening chapter presents the basic system of English as scholarly-traditional grammarians see it. The book may be used with profit even if Chapter 1 is ignored; but many instructors will want their students to become familiar with the organization and content of this chapter, which is designed to be a reference book within a reference book, at the beginning of the composition course. Students will find easy access to Chapter 1: the book's outside back cover indexes all the grammatical terms defined in that chapter.

Two different correction charts are provided for the instructor's use in guiding the student's revisions. One chart gives number-letter symbols according to the book's organization, with the name of the error or weakness accompanying the number-letter symbol. Instructors who use this chart will therefore make such marks as 3A, 10C, 22D, and so forth on the student's paper, and the student will know which section to refer to for guidance. This chart can also be used more generally, as when the instructor uses the number 10 to indicate an error in the use of the comma without specifying which rule has been violated.

The other chart is composed of traditional symbols, such as *agr, DM, W,* and so on, with the full name of the error following the symbol. The section of the handbook devoted to that error is identified in parentheses after the name of the error. Thus instructors who do not want to use number-letter symbols have a traditional correction chart available to them. The student will find the systems equally usable.

Most of the examples in the text are from student writing. Those that are not are nevertheless typical of problems that appear in student papers. The corrections address themselves only to the particular error and do not try to improve the sentence in other ways. To change more than the error under discussion might well distract the student. Every example is clearly labeled *wrong, right, poor style,* and so on, to reduce the possibility of confusion.

Two sections of the book may be called glossaries. Section 16G is composed of homophones—such as *course* and *coarse*—and other words that are often confused in spelling but not in meaning. Section 22B is composed of words often confused in meaning—such as *infer* and *imply*—and these are listed in the index. Both correction charts allow the instructor to refer the student to the glossaries.

ENNO KLAMMER

Introduction
to the Student

A Brief Handbook of English, Second Edition, is a guide to usage and grammar that will help you improve the conciseness, clarity, and correctness of your writing. It avoids minor points and long, complicated quibbles about what *could* be done under certain circumstances. Instead, it gives short, straightforward directions and clear examples of constructions and expressions that are correct and that will work effectively for you. You may choose to begin at page one and read to the end. More likely, you will look up various items that puzzle you or that your instructor directs you to study. Even when you are not using the book to revise one of your papers, you may use it to look up rules of punctuation, capitalization, spelling, and so on, so that your work will require less revision.

Skim through the book and become familiar with its organization and content. Knowing where to look is often as important as knowing what to do, especially at the outset. An index, two correction charts, and a list of grammatical terms will help you find what you want to know.

Start with the index as your most valuable tool. Each item of the text is listed at least once; some are under several headings. If, for example, you are puzzled about whether to place a period before or after closing quotation marks, look up *Period* in the index. The entry refers you to general information about periods, but it also lists *inside quotation marks* and the section and page (13E:120) where you will find the explanation you are looking for. (You'll also find the same reference under *Quotation marks, periods and commas within.*) Or suppose your instructor has marked DM (for "dangling modifier") next to one of your sentences. The entry *Dangling modifier* refers you to the pages in Chapter 23 where you can learn what a dangling modifier is and how to correct it.

Another useful tool is the correction chart on the inside front cover. It lists the information that appears in the table of contents and will help you to locate materials quickly. Notice that each page of the text itself shows the section number and letter (for example, 16D) in the upper corners of the pages; page numbers appear in the lower corners. The second correction chart is on the inside back cover. This chart directs you to sections in the text that treat common flaws in writing. When you revise your work, read whole sections so that by understanding general principles, rather than correcting only isolated errors, you can write your next essay satisfactorily.

The alphabetical list of grammatical terms on the outside back cover provides a quick reference to Chapter 1, "The Basic System of English Grammar." Although you will probably not be required to master this chapter all at once, read through it quickly to see what information it contains and how that information is organized. Thus if you need to find out what, say, a conjunctive adverb is, you can refer to the index on the back cover and then to the page in Chapter 1 that clearly explains what a conjunctive adverb is.

Contents

2

Sentence Fragments 37

3

Comma Splices and

Run-Together Sentences 43

4

Misused Modifiers 48

5

Pronoun Case Forms   55

6

Subject-Verb Agreement   63

7

Shifts   72

8

Verb Forms   79

SECTION TWO

PUNCTUATION AND MECHANICS   87

9

End Punctuation   89

10

The Comma   92

SECTION THREE
SPELLING   135

15
Spelling Rules   137

16
Spelling Lists   149

17

Capitalization 160

18

The Apostrophe 168

19

The Hyphen   174

SECTION FOUR

DICTION   179

20

Appropriate Word Choice   181

21

Exact Word Choice   188

SECTION SIX
THE RESEARCH PAPER 244

27
The Research Paper 245

SECTION ONE

GRAMMAR

1

Introduction:
The Basic System
of English Grammar

Since this text is a reference book, you will not be studying or referring to its chapters in sequence. Instead, on any particular day you may refer first to, say, Chapter 24, then Chapter 3, then Chapter 12, and so on. Thus you need to know some basic grammatical terms before you begin to use this book. This introductory chapter contains simple definitions, with brief examples, of the basic terms you need to know in order to use this book with ease and profit. Probably you already know some of these terms, and maybe all of them, but here they are for your reference, review, or study, should your teacher suggest that. Think of this chapter as a reference book within a reference book. Become familiar with it now, and refer to it for help whenever problems arise in your writing. All of the important terms in it are listed alphabetically with page references on the outside back cover.

1A PARTS OF SPEECH

Our language is composed of words, and each word is a part of speech. We recognize words as particular parts of speech by their form or their function, or both. Parts of speech have characteristic forms and functions: nouns serve as subjects and complements, adjectives modify nouns and pronouns, and so on. Yet in actual sentences, nouns and even verbs sometimes modify nouns. Thus parts of speech must be classified by **function** as well as by **form.** Examples:

ADJECTIVE MODIFYING NOUN: a **tall** lamp
NOUN MODIFYING NOUN: a **table** lamp
VERB MODIFYING NOUN: a **reading** lamp
DETERMINER MODIFYING NOUN: **my** lamp

Knowing that parts of speech may be classified by form and by function will help you use some chapters in this book more profitably. Further illustration of this dual classification, with names of the parts of speech by function, will be given in Section 1E.

The four parts of speech by form that carry the vast bulk of meaning in our language—**nouns, verbs, adjectives,** and **adverbs**—are known as **content words.** They will be defined next. Since these parts of speech are difficult to define, we will briefly discuss several characteristics of each. After a little practice you will come to have a natural feeling for which words are nouns, verbs, adjectives, and adverbs, if you do not already.

1A1 Nouns

A noun is the name of anything that exists or that you can think of. Thus such "names" as *apple, boot, car, chaos, love,* and *time* are nouns.

The form of almost every noun changes when it names more than one (plural) or shows possession (possessive) or both. Examples:

one **shot**   two **shots**
one **game**   two **games**
one **kiss**   two **kisses**
one **ox**   two **oxen**
one **child**   two **children**

BUT:

one **sheep**   two **sheep**

the **boy's** cap (only one boy had a cap)
the **boys'** caps (all the boys had caps)
the **Harrises'** anniversary (both of them celebrated)

Almost all nouns can be meaningfully preceded by one of the indefinite articles, *a* or *an;* or by the definite article, *the;* or by a possessive word such as *my, your,* or *John's.* Examples:

a **drink**   the **whisky**   Fred's **pride**
my **love**   her **hose**   Julia's **devotion**

Do not let intervening words—as in *a crisp, sweet apple*—keep you from understanding how *a, an, the, my,* and so on announce the presence of a noun.

Finally, certain word endings, or suffixes, added to other parts of speech form nouns. (Such suffixes are occasionally added to nouns also.) Note that adding such suffixes may sometimes change the spelling and pronunciation of the original word. Here are the most common of these nouns, with the suffixes in boldface:

mile + **age** = mileage
deny + **al** = denial
appear + **ance** = appearance
assist + **ant** = assistant
beg + **ar** = beggar
dull + **ard** = dullard
purify + **cation** = purification
secret + **cy** = secrecy
king + **dom** = kingdom
refer + **ee** = referee
superintend + **ent** = superintendent

advise + **er** = adviser
China + **ese** = Chinese
boy + **hood** = boyhood
just + **ice** = justice
act + **ion** = action
social + **ism** = socialism
commune + **ist** = communist
labor + **ite** = laborite
active + **ity** = activity
achieve + **ment** = achievement
lovely + **ness** = loveliness
counsel + **or** = counselor
slave + **ry** = slavery
kin + **ship** = kinship
dissent + **sion** = dissension
introduce + **tion** = introduction
fail + **ure** = failure

These word endings are known as **noun-forming suffixes.**

Proper nouns name particular persons, places, things, or ideas; they are capitalized wherever they occur in sentences (see Chapter 17).

the **building**	BUT	the Empire State **Building**
a **college**	BUT	Colorado **College**
an **ocean**	BUT	the Arctic **Ocean**

Knowledge of all the above characteristics of nouns will help you in identifying this part of speech.

1A2   Verbs

Verbs are words that express an action or a state of being. Usually, a verb gives an indication of the time of occurrence of the action or state of being. This indication is called tense. For example, the noun

a fight

expresses an action but no time of occurrence. But in

> José **will fight** fairly

or

> Sara **fights** viciously,

the same word used as a verb specifies a time of occurrence. (Note that a verb may be one word or more than one word. In the first sentence, "will fight" is the verb.)

Verbs, however, are most easily identified by form. With a very few exceptions, every verb in English has an *ing* form (called present participle) and a singular, present-tense form ending in *s* or *es*. Every verb also has either a regular (*ed*) or irregular past-tense and past-participle form. Thus virtually every English verb will fit this framework (called a paradigm):

infinitive	third-person singular, present tense	past tense	present participle	past participle
to hug	hugs	hugged	hugging	hugged
to break	breaks	broke	breaking	broken

Use the present participle when the word in front of it is a form of the auxiliary *be;* use the past participle when the auxiliary is *have, has,* or *had.*

> she **is** walk**ing**   she **has** walk**ed**
> they **were** notic**ing**   they **had** notic**ed**

For proper use of this text you need to know the three categories of verbs and three of their special functions. The three categories of verbs are as follows:

a. Transitive verbs A transitive verb is an action verb that, in a sentence, takes a direct object; that is, the action is performed on someone or something. Examples, with the direct object underlined:

TRANSITIVE VERBS: Lucy **smokes** cigars.
The pilot **worked** the controls.
Al **reads** magazines.

b. Intransitive verbs   An intransitive verb is an action verb that, in a sentence, does not have a direct object. The subject performs an action without anybody or anything receiving the action. Examples:

INTRANSITIVE VERBS: Howard **smokes** too often.
This can opener **works** strangely.
Al **reads** to his children.

Modifiers, such as the adverbs *too often* and *strangely* and the prepositional phrase *to his children,* do not prevent a verb from being intransitive. The noun *children* is the object of the preposition *to,* not a direct object of the verb.

Note that some verbs can be transitive in some sentences and intransitive in others.

c. Linking verbs   Linking verbs are state-of-being verbs, such as *to be, to seem, to appear, to become, to look, to taste, to feel, to sound, to remain.* Linking verbs are followed either by a predicate noun, which tells what the subject is or seems to be, or by a predicate adjective, which describes the subject. Examples:

LINKING VERBS: Julius **is** a weirdo.
Mr. Merle **became** dogcatcher.
Shirley **looks** pregnant.
Barry **remained** calm.

Weirdo and *dogcatcher* are predicate nouns, and *pregnant* and *calm* are predicate adjectives.

Some verbs can function as either intransitive, transitive, or linking. Examples:

TRANSITIVE: George **grew** a beard. (direct object *beard*)
INTRANSITIVE: The tree **grew** slowly. (no direct object)
LINKING: My date **grew** restless. (predicate adjective *restless*)

Linking verbs cause some special writing problems, which are covered in later chapters.

The three special functions of verbs that you need to know are the following:

d. Tense Tense is the function of verbs that specifies time of occurrence. The tense system in English is immensely complex, but to use this book you need to know only whether a verb form contains one of the past, present, or future tenses. Examples:

PAST TENSES: My horse **vanished** last night.
The cops **had left** before I **returned.**

PRESENT TENSES: I **am telling** you the truth.
Shelley usually **studies** after midnight.

FUTURE TENSES: Times **will get** better.
Maurice **is going to plead** guilty.

e. Voice Voice has to do with whether a subject performs or receives an action. Only action verbs have voice. If the subject performs the action in a sentence, the verb and sentence are said to be in the **active voice.** Example:

ACTIVE VOICE: Benny **mugged** an old man for six pennies.

If the subject receives the action, the verb and sentence are said to be in the **passive voice.** Example:

PASSIVE VOICE: An old man **was mugged** for six pennies.

If the doer of the action in a passive-voice sentence is mentioned, he is named in a *by* phrase; e.g., *by Benny* could be attached to the preceding example sentence. A passive-voice verb always has a form of *to be* in it.

f. Mood Mood is the function of a verb that expresses the speaker's attitude toward the factuality or likelihood of what he says. The **indicative mood** expresses a fact or what is believed to be a fact. Example:

INDICATIVE MOOD: Ricky **makes** more money stealing than
I **do** working.

The **subjunctive mood** indicates condition contrary to fact, or doubt, potentiality, desirability, obligation, and other such nonfactual concepts. Examples:

SUBJUNCTIVE MOOD: I wish I **were** a member of the Realities.

I suggested that he **keep** quiet. (Note that *keeps* won't function here properly even though *he* is singular.)

You **should marry** a second wife.

The **imperative mood** states a request or command. Usually *you,* the subject of imperative statements, is omitted. Examples:

IMPERATIVE MOOD: **Get** off my back.

Scatter before we're caught.

There are other functions of verbs, but the foregoing are the ones that have to do with writing problems discussed in later chapters.

1A3 Adjectives

An adjective is a describing word; it describes (or modifies) a noun or pronoun by telling *which one, what kind,* and so on. But other parts of speech—such as the noun *comedian* and the verb *stumbles*—also carry an element of description. Thus *adjective* is very hard to define. But an understanding of the following characteristics of adjectives will give you a feel for identifying them.

First, almost all adjectives can be **compared** with *er* (or *more*) and *est* (or *most*). Examples:

stem	comparative form	superlative form
sweet	sweeter	sweetest
beautiful	more beautiful	most beautiful

But since adverbs also can be compared, more is needed to identify adjectives by form. Thus if a word can be compared *and* (1) can have *ly* added to make an adverb *or* (2) can have *ness* added to make a noun, it is an adjective. Examples:

clear	clearer	clearest	clearly
mean	meaner	meanest	meanness

Words fitting these two requirements are always adjectives. In comparing some adjectives (or adverbs) *more* and *most* are used instead of *er* and *est* solely to make the word sound smooth rather than awkward. *Beautifulest* is awkward, while *most beautiful* is smooth. The comparative (*er*) and superlative (*est*) forms of *good* and *well* are the irregular *better* and *best;* of *bad* and *ill* they are the irregular *worse* and *worst.*

Another easy test to help you get the feel of the adjective is to see that adjectives fit this pattern (any common noun can be used instead of *student*):

That _____ student is very _____ .

Examples:

That **bright** student is very **bright.**
That **obscene** joke is very **obscene.**

Almost always when a word fits this pattern it is an adjective by form, and almost all adjectives will fit the pattern.

Here is another easy test to identify adjectives:

He (she, it) seems _____

Virtually every word *except a noun* that will fit this slot is an adjective. Examples:

He seems **up-tight.**
She seems **virtuous.**
It seems **dead.**

An understanding of this structural position of the adjective will improve your ability to recognize that part of speech automatically.

Finally, we use a number of suffixes to convert other parts of speech (and occasionally other adjectives) into adjectives. Here are the most common, with the suffixes in boldface:

read + **able** = readable
person + **al** = personal
Africa + **an** = African
resist + **ant** = resistant

fortune + **ate** = fortunate
conserve + **ative** = conservative
exist + **ent** = existent
sin + **ful** = sinful
athlete + **ic** = athletic
boy + **ish** = boyish
assert + **ive** = assertive
mercy + **less** = merciless
bird + **like** = birdlike
lone + **ly** = lonely
prohibit + **ory** = prohibitory
courage + **ous** = courageous
quarrel + **some** = quarrelsome
shine + **y** = shiny

These word endings are known as **adjective-forming suffixes.** Understanding them will help you develop a feel for identifying adjectives. Be sure to note that the suffix *ly* forms only a few adjectives; in most cases that suffix changes an adjective into an adverb. If a word ending in *ing* or *ed*—such as *interesting* or *excited*—can be modified by *very,* it is an adjective.

1A4   Adverbs

Like the adjective, the adverb is a describing word. Its most common function is to describe (or modify) a verb, telling how, when, or where. (Also, adverbs sometimes modify adjectives and other adverbs.) The so-called "pure" adverbs are those that are formed from adjectives by the addition of the suffix *ly.* Examples:

adjective	*adverb*
rapid	rapidly
sweet	sweetly
loving	lovingly
excited	excitedly

Like adjectives, such adverbs can be compared. Examples:

stem	comparative form	superlative form
bitterly	more bitterly	most bitterly
happily	more happily	most happily

This is the easy way to recognize most English adverbs, but you should be careful not to confuse the few *ly* adjectives—*kindly, lovely, friendly, timely*—with adverbs.

The difference between adjectives and adverbs is illustrated in these two sentences:

ADJECTIVE: John looked **curious.**
ADVERB: John looked **curiously.**

The first sentence (with *looked* as a linking verb) describes the appearance of John. The second (with *looked* as an intransitive verb) tells the manner in which John looked at something.

English also has a number of so-called "flat" adverbs that do not end in *ly* but that do usually modify verbs. Most of them express either time or place. The most common ones are *soon, never, often, there, here, upward, well* (which is also an adjective), *inside, now, seldom, always, somewhere, behind,* and *above.*

A useful fact to know about adverbs is that most of them express **time, place,** or **manner** and thus can have the words *then, there,* or *thus* substituted for them. Examples:

I'll come **sometime.** = I'll come **then.**
I can't find the jam **anywhere.** = I can't find the jam **there.**
She smiled **wickedly.** = She smiled **thus.**

However, words and word groups that are not adverbs by form also modify verbs, and they may meaningfully have *then, there,* or *thus* substituted for them. Examples:

We'll call **at ten o'clock.** = then   (*At ten o'clock* is a prepositional phrase.)
Cheryl came **home.** = there   (*Home* is a noun.)
Hemingway wrote **standing.** = thus   (*Standing* is a verb.)

In Section 1E we will make modification clearer, but understanding the above characteristics of adverbs will give you a feel for identifying them. Some important writing problems are concerned with the distinction between adjectives and adverbs.

1A5 Structure Words

The vast majority of words in English are nouns, verbs, adjectives, and adverbs. As content words, they are **open classes,** which means that new words (or new definitions of old words) enter these classes frequently, thus expanding the English vocabulary. A much smaller number of words, but a larger number of parts of speech, are called **structure words.** Even though most of these words carry some meaning, their chief function is to provide a framework for arranging the many nouns, verbs, adjectives, and adverbs into meaningful sentences. The structure words all belong to **closed classes,** because new ones very rarely enter the language. There are many kinds of structure words, and there is much overlapping in the groups. (That is, one word, such as *that,* may belong to several groups.) Their grammatical behavior is complex. We will mention and briefly define only those of which you need an elementary knowledge in order to use this text as a reference handbook. What follows is only a very small part of the total grammar of structure words, the part that will be useful to you.

a. Determiners Words that signal that a noun is coming are called determiners. They determine something about the nature of the noun that follows. Sometimes two determiners precede a noun. A few single determiners consist of two words. Here are examples of the chief determiners:

a bottle	**no** money
an oyster	**some** disease
the grape	**all** prisons
my beer	**every** chance
John's hangover	**such a** pity
this remedy	**all the** excuses

The words in boldface may be thought of as noun markers. Any **noun marker** like these is a determiner. Of course other words may come between the determiner and its noun, as in *a silly old man.*

Incidentally, the list above shows how parts of speech may be labeled differently as their functions differ. While *John's* is a determiner here, *John* is commonly a noun; *all* and *some* can be pronouns, and so on.

b. Prepositions A preposition is a kind of connective that shows a relationship between two words. The second word is usually a noun or noun substitute that functions as the object of the preposition and helps form a prepositional phrase. (Prepositional phrases are discussed in more detail in Section 1C1.) Examples, with the prepositions in boldface and the prepositional phrases underlined (notice that a pronoun as the object of a preposition changes its form to the objective case):

the man **with** the hoe	different **from** us
the time **of** day	do it **for** me
a trip **to** the islands	conducted **by** the composer

You would be very hard pressed to give a clear definition of *with, from, of,* and *for* in these constructions; they are structure, not content, words. However, most prepositions do have some meaning. In using a number of the chapters of this text you will need to recognize prepositional phrases. Here are the most common single-word prepositions:

above	besides	into	through
across	between	like	till
after	beyond	near	to
along	but	of	toward(s)
among	by	off	under
around	down	on	until
at	during	outside	upon
before	for	over	with
behind	from	past	within
below	in	save	without
beside	inside	since	

We also have compound prepositions in English, of which the following are the most common:

ahead of	contrary to	instead of
apart from	due to	on account to
as for	for the sake of	out of
as well as	in addition to	owing to
aside from	in back of	rather than
away from	in case of	together with
because of	in front of	up at
belonging to	in place of	up on
by means of	in spite of	up to
by way of	inside of	with regard to

Some of these compound prepositions—as in the construction *in addition to the money*—can be analyzed as forming two prepositional phrases rather than one phrase with a compound preposition.

c. Verb auxiliaries   Many verbs are composed of two or more words, the last word being the main verb and the others being auxiliaries that specify tense and other meanings. Examples, with the auxiliaries in boldface:

may go	**will** go
have been going	**will be** gone
could have gone	**should have been** going

The number of possible combinations of auxiliaries in English verb forms is enormous. Fortunately, in order to use this text, you need only recognize auxiliaries, not understand their complex grammar.

The verbs *to be, to do,* and *to have* have meanings in English and can function as sentence verbs. But forms of these verbs also function as auxiliaries, with their meanings being entirely different from their meanings as regular verbs. For example, in

I **have** some beans,

have has the meaning of *possess.* But in

I **have** roasted some beans,

have has no such meaning. It is an auxiliary verb that helps to convey tense. The case is similar with *to be* and *to do.* These forms of *to be, to do,* and *to have* function as verb auxiliaries:

> *to be:* be, am, is, are, was, were, being, *and* been
> *to do:* do, does, *and* did
> *to have:* has, have, having, *and* had

Examples:

> Joseph **has been** studying for an hour.
> Molly **does** respect her parents.

Another group of words is called **modal auxiliaries.** Although they are used with a main verb, they carry meaning of their own. The chief modal auxiliaries are the following:

can	may	must	shall	will
could	might	ought to	should	would

Examples:

> I **may** leave early, but you **ought to** help the committee.

The modals carry some tense meaning and also express subtle meanings of intent, possibility, obligation, and condition.

When any form of *be* is an auxiliary, the next verb will end in *ing;* when *have* is the auxiliary, the next verb form will be a past participle; and when *do* or any modal is the auxiliary, the following verb must be in its base form.

d. Coordinating connectives A coordinating connective joins two grammatical constructions equal in rank, such as two nouns, two prepositional phrases, or two independent clauses. Many of the chapters in this text will refer to such compound structures. Two classes of these connectives are to be identified:

Coordinating conjunctions (with two exceptions) may be used to join pairs of many kinds of constructions, from single words to independent clauses. (Clauses will be discussed more fully later in this chapter.) They are the following:

and	or	both . . . and
but	nor	not only . . . but (also)
yet	for	either . . . or
	so	neither . . . nor

For and *so* can be used to join only independent clauses. The two-part conjunctions are also called **correlatives.**

Conjunctive adverbs are coordinating connectives that join only independent clauses. When used, they require specific punctuation. They are the following:

accordingly	furthermore	otherwise
afterward(s)	hence	still
also	however	then
besides	later	therefore
consequently	moreover	thus
earlier	nevertheless	

Both kinds of coordinating connectives express such relationships as **contrast, cause-and-result, accumulation, conditions,** and **time.** When a coordinating connective joins two independent clauses, each could stand by itself as a full, complete sentence, for a sentence may begin with a coordinating connective (see Sections 3B and 12B).

e. Subordinating conjunctions A subordinating conjunction is a connective that expresses a relationship between two ideas that are not equal in rank. That is, one of the ideas can stand by itself as a sentence, but the idea introduced by the subordinating conjunction cannot. If it stood by itself, it would be a nonsentence, or a sentence fragment. Many words that are subordinating conjunctions in some sentence can be prepositions or other connectives in other sentences. You will recall that there is much overlapping of structure words in English. For reference, here is a list of subordinating conjunctions:

after	if	since
although	in case (that)	so long as
as	in order that	so (that)
as . . . as	in that	than
as if	inasmuch as	though
as long as	less than	unless
as soon as	like	until
as though	more than	when
because	no matter how	where
before	now that	whereas
even though	once	while
fewer than	provided (that)	

The subordinating conjunctions are very important words that express such adverbial relationships as **cause-and-result, contrast, condition, manner** or **method, purpose, time,** and **place.** To use this reference handbook fully, you need a basic understanding of them.

f. Pronouns A pronoun is defined as a word that stands for a noun, the noun being the pronoun's **antecedent.** But the English pronoun system is far more complex than that definition indicates. The pronoun system causes so many writing problems that it will be dealt with in several chapters of this book. Here, we will identify five kinds of pronouns: personal, relative, interrogative, demonstrative, and indefinite.

The **personal pronouns** have **case,** which means that they change their forms according to their use in sentences. There are three cases in English: (1) the **subjective,** (2) the **objective,** and (3) the **possessive.** Here are the case forms of the personal pronouns:

subjective case	*objective case*	*possessive case*
I	me	my, mine
you	you	your, yours
he	him	his
she	her	her, hers
it	it	its
we	us	our, ours
they	them	their, theirs

The personal pronouns also have **reflexive** forms, as follows:

myself	himself
ourselves	herself
yourself	itself
yourselves	themselves (not theirselves)

The chief **relative pronouns** are *who* (subjective case), *whom* (objective case), *whose* (possessive case), *which,* and *that.* (These last two do not have case.) A relative pronoun is used to connect (or relate) a dependent clause to a noun in another part of the sentence. Example:

There's the cop **who** busted me.

The antecedent of *who* is *cop. Who* introduces the clause and relates it to the preceding noun. Such dependent clauses that begin with a relative pronoun are called *relative clauses* or *adjective clauses.* Like adjectives, they modify a noun or pronoun by telling *which one* or *what kind.* The relative pronouns, then, are connectives; they join ideas to each other.

Sometimes a relative pronoun is not stated but is understood in a sentence. Example:

The course I like best is Marriage and Family Life.

The relative pronoun *that,* with *course* as its antecedent, is understood before *I.*

Who and *whom* are also **interrogative** (question-forming) pronouns. They pose a writing problem that is discussed in Section 5C.

The **demonstrative pronouns** are the "pointing" pronouns *this, that, these,* and *those.* They may be used with nouns (as determiners) or by themselves, with the nouns understood. Examples:

This pornography seems mild today.
That is the one I want.

In the second sentence, whatever subject is under discussion is understood after *that.*

This and *that* are also used in a more general way to refer to whole ideas. Examples:

RIGHT: I expected Professor Sneed to flunk me, and **that** is what he did.

RIGHT: We are out of cash again. **This** is getting to be a common occurrence.

In these examples, both *that* and *this* have whole ideas as their antecedents.

There is also a sizable group of words in English known as **indefinite pronouns.** They function as singular nouns but make indefinite reference to people or things.

one	nobody
no one	somebody
anyone	other
everyone	another
someone	one another
anybody	each other
each	anyone else (and
everybody	others with *else*)

g. Qualifiers   A small group of words that modify adjectives and adverbs are called qualifiers because they qualify, or limit in some way, the meaning of adjectives and adverbs. Some colloquial qualifiers, discussed in Section 20B, should be avoided in semiformal writing. (Most college writing may be classed as semiformal.) The chief qualifiers used in semiformal writing are the following:

very	somewhat	fairly	a little
rather	especially	wholly	quite

1B   SENTENCES

The parts of speech defined in Section 1A are variously arranged to form sentences. Every sentence is composed of a **subject** (what you want to talk about) and a **predicate** (what you want to say about the subject), and every predicate contains a verb that shows tense. A predicate may or may not contain a **complement,** which is a word or word group that completes a meaning begun in the verb. The chief complements are direct objects, indirect objects, predicate nouns, and predicate adjectives.

1B1 Subjects

The **subject** names the person, thing, or concept about which the rest of the sentence makes a statement. If the verb is in the active voice, the subject performs the action. If the verb is in the passive voice, the subject receives the action. If the verb is a linking verb, the subject is in the state of being that the verb expresses.

A simple test for determining the subject of a sentence is to ask *who* or *what* about the verb. Examples:

Our team won the championship. (Active verb)

Who won? *Our team,* which is therefore the subject.

The championship was won by our team. (Passive verb)

What was won? *The championship,* which is the subject.

Sally appears dazed. (*Appears* is a linking verb.)

Who appears? *Sally,* which is the subject.

Sometimes the subject is a noun with many modifiers. Such a noun and all of its modifiers together form the **complete subject.** Example:

Any high official of the United States government can be impeached.

Who can be impeached? *Any high official of the United States government,* which is the complete subject. The central noun (also known as the headword) in such a long subject is known as the **simple subject.** It—and it alone—controls the verb. Example:

Any member of a nudist camp that is affiliated with other camps can have free access to those camps too.

Who can have free access? *Any member,* which is the simple subject within the complete subject. (The complete subject is all of the words preceding *can have.*)

A good point to remember is that in the vast majority of English sentences the subject precedes the verb. Two rather frequent exceptions are sentences that begin with *there* and *it* as **expletives** (fillers without meaning). Examples, with the complete subjects in boldface:

> There is **no way to form a compound out of helium and hydrogen.**

What is? The whole boldfaced construction is, with *no way* as the simple subject.

> It is true **that Doug jilted Maggie.**

What is true? The whole boldfaced noun clause, which is the subject. (There is no single-word simple subject in such sentences.) Some writers do at times use inverted sentence order; but usually asking *who* or *what* about the verb will tell you the subject.

1B2 Predicates

The predicate of a sentence is the verb and its complement, if it has one, plus any modifiers (see Section 1E). Examples, with the predicates in boldface:

> The bee **stung Uncle Wilhelm.**
> Pete **can run very fast.**
> The young mother **screamed at the teenagers bullying her children.**

The headword in the predicate is always the verb (which may be one or more words). The verb must be what is called **finite,** that is, it must be a form that shows tense or time of action. Some examples of finite verbs are the following:

> Jess **has been going** to a psychiatrist for a year now.
> He **is profiting** from his treatment.
> His parents **aren't.**

Verb forms that cannot function as sentence verbs are known as **nonfinite.** They include present participles (ending in *ing*), past participles (often ending in *ed*), and infinitives (beginning with *to*). Some examples are *known, been gone,* and *having escaped.* The following groups of words are not sentences:

> We known about the fire
> Shirley been gone now for two days

The addition of verb auxiliaries that show the tense would make these verbs finite and make correct sentences:

> We **should have known** about the fire.
> Shirley **has been gone** now for two days.

Many predicates have **complements** of the verbs— that is, words or constructions that complete a meaning initiated in the verb. To use this book effectively, you need to understand only four kinds of complements:

a. Direct objects   A direct object is the person or thing that receives the action of a transitive verb. Examples:

DIRECT OBJECTS: Jonesy lit his **cigar.**
       The transcriber omitted an **expletive.**

A simple test for finding the direct object is to ask *who* or *what* after you state the subject and the verb. Jonesy lit what? He lit the cigar. *Cigar* is the direct object.

b. Indirect objects   An indirect object normally occurs only in conjunction with a direct object. It specifies the person or thing to or for whom the action is performed. Examples:

INDIRECT OBJECTS: Hortense gave **me** a kiss.
       The deacon told **the preacher** a lie.

Kiss and *lie* are direct objects. Indirect objects can always be converted into prepositional phrases beginning with *to* or *for.* Example:

> The deacon told a lie **to the preacher.**

In this sentence the indirect object has been replaced by a prepositional phrase.

c. Predicate nouns A predicate noun follows a linking verb and renames the subject in different terms. Examples:

PREDICATE NOUNS: Elsie remained **chairperson** of the
                 English Department.
                 Susie is a **sweetheart**.

d. Predicate adjectives A predicate adjective follows a linking verb and describes the subject. Examples:

PREDICATE ADJECTIVES: The moon is **bright** tonight.
                       Julio became **bitter** later on.

In all the examples above, the complements plus the verbs and modifiers form the sentence predicates.

1B3 Kinds of Sentences

Though there seems to be an infinity of different kinds of English sentences, for simplicity we will identify four types.

a. A simple sentence is one that contains only one independent clause and no dependent clause. (See Section 1D for a description of clauses.) Even though various kinds of phrases carrying additional ideas may be in such a sentence, it is still called simple. Examples:

Glass is a noncrystalline substance.
Without any hesitation, I strode into the panther's cage.

Regardless of its length, a simple sentence has only one subject and one predicate, though either the subject or the predicate or both may have more than one element (see Section 6D). Examples:

COMPOUND SUBJECT: **Tom, Dick,** and **Harry** / met at my place.
COMPOUND PREDICATE: We / **drank beer** and **played records.**
COMPOUND SUBJECT AND COMPOUND PREDICATE:
    May and **Joan** / **came over** and **stayed awhile.**

,45,000

LIBRARY
College of St. Francis   25
JOLIET, ILLINOIS

b. A compound sentence is one composed of two or more independent clauses but no dependent clauses. Examples, with the independent clauses in boldface:

> **We didn't care about breaking the speed limit,** but **the liquor store had already closed.**
> **The sun and moon appear to be about the same size;** however, **they are really vastly different in size.**

A compound sentence has at least two subjects and two predicates, one each in each distinct clause.

c. A complex sentence has one independent clause and one or more dependent clauses. Examples, with the dependent clauses in boldface:

> **While Ruthie kept guard,** I climbed through the transom.
> I won't vote for Mr. Huston **because he slandered minority groups.**
> **If it rains,** we'll call off our race, **since the roadway would be too slippery for our tires.**

d. A compound-complex sentence contains at least two independent clauses and at least one dependent clause. Examples, with the dependent clauses in boldface:

> **If the weather is fair,** we will go on our hunting trip, and I expect us to find much game.
> **Since I could see his hat on the table,** I knew of the intruder's presence, but I made no move **in case he had a pistol.**

This traditional fourfold classification of sentence types does not tell the whole truth about the great variety of structure in English sentences, but it is a useful starting point.

1C PHRASES

A phrase is a group of words that function as a unit but that do not have a subject and predicate. You need to understand three kinds of phrases in order to use this book fully.

1C1 Prepositional Phrases

A prepositional phrase begins with a preposition and closes with the object of the preposition, usually a noun or pronoun. If the object of a preposition is a pronoun, such a pronoun is in the objective case. Examples:

PREPOSITIONAL PHRASES: The girl **in the bikini** standing **next to him** was invited **as an additional guest.**

Prepositional phrases are used as modifiers, like adjectives and adverbs.

1C2 Verbal Phrases

A verbal phrase is a verb form plus various other words that go with it to form a unit. Many different nonfinite verb forms can be headwords in verb phrases, but to use this book you need not know their names. You need only to recognize that a verb form is the headword of the phrase and that the phrase is a unit. Examples:

VERBAL PHRASES: The man **to see about tickets** is Scalper Joe.

Realizing we were trapped, we meekly surrendered.

Known for her generosity, Caroline was often imposed upon.

Jogging every morning helped me lose ten pounds.

Several kinds of errors in sentence structure and punctuation involve verbal phrases.

1C3   Noun Phrases

A noun phrase is composed of a noun headword plus all its modifiers. Examples:

NOUN PHRASES: **A list of students serving as student-body officers** was posted in the library.
A number of spectators at the construction site offered much advice to the workers.

The headwords in these phrases are *list* and *number;* they govern the whole phrases. You will need to understand the nature of noun phrases to deal with subject-verb agreement.

1D   CLAUSES

A **clause** is a construction that has a subject and predicate (see Sections 1B1 and 1B2). Clauses are either independent or dependent.

1D1   Independent Clauses

An **independent clause** is in effect a simple sentence. It is a clause that can stand alone, beginning with a capital letter and ending with a period or question mark. Even when it appears in a complex or compound sentence, such a clause that *could* stand alone is still called an independent clause. The material in Sections 1B1 and 1B2 gives you information that applies to independent clauses as well as to sentences.

1D2   Dependent Clauses

Dependent clauses are like independent clauses in having a subject and a predicate containing a finite verb. They differ in that they begin with subordinating connectives, which keep them from standing alone as complete sentences. *Grammatically,* a dependent clause depends on the rest of the sentence, but, since it has a subject and predicate, it contains a full unit of meaning. There are three kinds of dependent clauses.

a. Adjective clauses generally begin with one of these relative pronouns, which serve as subordinating connectives: *who, whom, whose, which,* and *that.* Like adjectives, an adjective clause usually modifies a noun or pronoun. In the examples below, each adjective clause modifies the noun it follows.

ADJECTIVE CLAUSES: The guest **who arrives last** will receive a booby prize.

A man **whose wife is beautiful** is always worried.

We elected Sneedby, **who paid two dollars a vote.**

I voted for Scraggs, **to whom I owed a debt.**

The subjects and predicates of these adjective clauses are as follows:

who / arrives last
whose wife / is beautiful
who / paid two dollars a vote
I / owed a debt to whom (to Scraggs)

Occasionally an adjective clause can modify the whole idea of a sentence or word group, in which case it must begin with *which.* In this example, the adjective clause, in boldface, modifies the whole idea of the independent clause:

The catcher of our team batted .406 this year, **which set a new local record.**

An understanding of adjective clauses is especially important in knowing how to punctuate correctly (see Section 10F).

b. Adverb clauses begin with one of the subordinating conjunctions listed on page 19. The subordinating conjunction expresses a relationship between the adverb clause and, usually, some other whole idea. Like simple adverbs, many such adverb clauses modify the verb in another clause. Examples:

ADVERB CLAUSES: **If you drink,** I will drive.
I proposed to you **because you are rich.**
You will marry me **because I am handsome.**

The subjects and predicates of these adverb clauses are as follows:

you / drink
you / are rich
I / am handsome

The subordinating conjunctions *if* and *because* make the clauses dependent, or keep them from standing alone as complete sentences.

  c. Noun clauses begin with *that* (a meaningless subordinating connective), with *what,* with *whatever, whoever, whichever,* with a relative pronoun, or with a subordinating conjunction. (Only a few of the subordinating conjunctions can begin noun clauses.) The distinctive characteristic of noun clauses is that they function as nouns in sentences—usually as subjects or direct objects. The best way to test for a noun clause is to see that either *someone* or *something* can be substituted for it. Examples:

NOUN CLAUSES: I known **that you love me.** (I know something.)
When you leave is no concern of mine. (Something is no concern of mine.)
Whoever buys the beer chooses the music we play. (Someone chooses the music we play.)

The subjects and predicates of these noun clauses are as follows:

you / love me
you / leave
whoever / buys the beer

The *that, when,* and *whoever* prevent the clauses from standing as complete sentences.

A number of the following chapters, especially those on punctuation, will deal with dependent clauses.

1E MODIFIERS

A **modifier** is a word or word group that describes, limits, or adds to another word or word group. For example, if to the phrase *a shirt* we add the modifier *blue* to get *a blue shirt,* we have (1) described the shirt to a degree; (2) limited the shirt, since all non-blue shirts are now excluded; and (3) in a sense, added to the shirt, since we have told something about it that formerly we did not know. This all seems simple, but actually modification is one of the most complex aspects of grammar. You need to know some of the aspects of modification in order to deal with many writing problems treated in the following chapters.

There are three general kinds of modifiers. In discussing them we return to the fact that parts of speech are classified by form and by function. Thus some words may function as adjectives or adverbs even though they are classified as other parts of speech. The three general kinds of modifiers are **adjectivals, adverbials,** and **sentence modifiers.**

1E1 Adjectivals

Any word or word group that modifies a noun or pronoun is by function an adjectival. Here are examples of various kinds of adjectivals. The adjectival is in boldface and the noun it modifies is underlined.

> the **tastiest** <u>biscuit</u>   [*Tastiest* is an adjective.]
> This <u>cloth</u> feels **smooth.**   [*Smooth* is an adjective.]
> a **paper** <u>tiger</u>   [*Paper* is a noun functioning as an adjectival.]
> a **running** <u>thief</u>   [*Running* is a verb functioning as an adjectival.]

the apartment **below** [*Below* is an adverb functioning as an adjectival.]

the go-go dancer **on stage in the nightclub** [*On stage* and *in the nightclub* are prepositional phrases functioning as adjectivals. *On stage* modifies *dancer* and *in the nightclub* modifies *stage.*]

the girl **not wearing a bikini** [The verbal phrase functions as an adjectival.]

Being exhausted, Joe took a nap. [The verbal phrase functions as an adjectival.]

Dr. Smale, **whose specialty is urology** [The adjective clause functions as an adjectival.]

a time **when all chickens are asleep.** [The adverb clause functions as an adjectival.]

Although most of the constructions in boldface are not adjectives, they are all adjectivals by function because they modify nouns.

1E2 Adverbials

Any word or word group that modifies a verb, adjective, or another adverb is an adverbial by function. Most adverbials answer the questions *where, when,* or *how.* Here are examples of various kinds of adverbials. The adverbial in each instance is in boldface and the verb it modifies is underlined:

to peer **cautiously** [*Cautiously* is an adverb.]

arrived **yesterday** [*Yesterday* is a noun functioning as an adverbial.]

If you study **long,** you study **wrong.** [*Long* and *wrong* are adjectives functioning as adverbials.]

frozen **by the north wind** [The prepositional phrase functions as an adverbial.]

to eat **standing** [*Standing* is a verb functioning as an adverbial.]

I studied hard **to improve my grades.** [The verb phrase functions as an adverbial.]

smoking **where it is forbidden** [The adverb clause functions as an adverbial.]

All of the constructions in boldface are adverbials because they modify verbs.

1E3 Sentence Modifiers

In some sentences a modifier modifies not a single word but a whole idea. Then it is a sentence modifier, usually set off from the rest of the sentence by a comma. Here are examples of sentence modifiers, which are in boldface:

> **Happily,** Tweed did not die. [*Happily* is an adverb modifying the whole sentence. Note how different in meaning this sentence is from "Tweed did not die happily," in which *happily* is an adverbial modifying *die.*]
>
> **Under the circumstances,** we should engage in plea bargaining. [The prepositional phrase modifies the whole idea.]
>
> **Strictly speaking,** the purchase of a new car is not an investment. [The verbal phrase modifies the whole idea.]
>
> We invested in common stock, **which is a good way to go broke fast.** [The dependent clause modifies the first idea.]

In determining what a word or word group modifies, the best approach is to ask *what goes with what.* In Sections 1E1 and 1E2, if you will ask this question about the examples, you will see that the boldface construction goes with what is underlined.

1F APPOSITIVES

Basically, an **appositive** is a noun repeater; that is, it renames in different words the noun it is **in apposition to.** It gives more information about that noun. An appositive may be a single word, a phrase, or a clause. Examples of appositives, with the appositive in boldface and the noun it is in apposition to underlined:

> Neutron stars, **heavenly bodies with a diameter of only a**

few miles, were discovered in the 1970s. [The apposi-
tive is a noun phrase.]
The <u>British writer</u> **John Wilson** may receive a Nobel Prize.
[The appositive is a noun.]
The <u>belief</u> **that like produces like** is an old superstition.
[The appositive is a noun clause.]
Her <u>first love</u>—**eating wild mushrooms**—was her last act.
[The appositive is a verbal phrase.]

Sometimes an appositive is in apposition to a whole idea.
Example:

<u>He conceded the election</u>, a **gesture** his backers disap-
proved of.

The appositive in boldface is in apposition to the underlined sentence. Occasionally appositives are introduced
by such connectives as *that is, namely,* and *or.* Example:

Vibrissae, or **whiskers,** grow on the faces of all species of
cats and seals.

Whiskers is in apposition to *vibrissae.*
    Appositives involve important aspects of punctuation
and will be considered further in Section Two.

1G   COORDINATION

Coordination means the joining of two or more sentence
parts or independent clauses so that they are equal in
rank. This grammatical function, which involves problems
in punctuation and sentence structure, usually calls for
one of the coordinating connectives discussed in Section
1A5d. Parts are said to be **compounded** when they are
coordinated. When three or more coordinated parts appear, we speak of them as **items in a series.** Examples
of coordination:

Updike, Faulkner, and **Hemingway** are American authors.
Riding horses, drinking whisky, and **writing novels** were
William Faulkner's favorite pastimes.

The expressions in boldface are equal in rank.

1H SUBORDINATION

Subordination means that one sentence part is unequal in rank to another part. Prepositional phrases and verbal phrases are always subordinate to the words or ideas they modify. Subordinate clauses are usually introduced by one of the subordinating conjunctions discussed in Section 1A5e or by a relative pronoun or by *that* or *what.* Also, any kind of sentence modifier is a subordinate construction. Example of subordination, with the subordinated clause in boldface:

Vodka is intoxicating, **though it is free of fusel oils.**

If the *though,* which produces subordination, is changed to *but,* coordination results:

Vodka is intoxicating, but it is free of fusel oils.

Now the clauses are equal in rank.

Coordination and subordination are involved in various aspects of sentence structure and punctuation. An understanding of coordination and subordination is important for expressing meaning precisely.

1I AMBIGUITY

An important term in grammar is **ambiguity.** This means that a sentence has two possible meanings, often without a clue to show the reader which meaning is intended. Examples of ambiguity:

How would you like to see a model home?
Bathing beauties can be fun.
During my college career I had thirty odd teachers.
I will lose no time in reading your manuscript.

Ambiguities can be entertaining, but usually ambiguity is a grave weakness in writing.

The foregoing are explanations of the basics of English grammar that pertain to the writing problems that are discussed in the rest of this reference handbook. You may not need to make much use of this introductory chapter, but it is here for you, and it may at times answer pressing questions or give you insights that will improve the quality of your writing.

2

Sentence Fragments

A good writer needs to have **sentence sense** to avoid writing in **sentence fragments,** or nonsentences. Chapter 1 shows that every sentence must have at least one independent clause containing a well-formed subject and a well-formed predicate; in addition, many sentences have various phrases and subordinate clauses as modifiers. Sentence sense is the ability to recognize that a construction is either a complete sentence that can stand alone, or a sentence fragment that should not stand alone. The person with sentence sense automatically composes in complete sentences, but one who does not have full sentence sense often makes serious errors in writing. These errors are discussed in this chapter and Chapter 3.

Sentence sense is largely intuitive. Many people easily develop sentence sense without fully understanding just why they have it. Some other people have much difficulty in developing it. Generally, people who study grammar, which is compactly presented in our first chapter, develop sentence sense more easily than do those who are unaware of the nature of grammar.

The whole problem of sentence sense is complex and involves oddities. For example, consider the following construction:

While the professor explained the theory of relativity

Every word (except possibly *while*) in that construction contains its own full meaning without reference to a preceding sentence; yet the construction is not a sentence and should not be entered into writing as though it were a sentence. On the other hand, many sentences that are *grammatically* complete don't make much sense unless you know what an earlier sentence has said; they draw their meaning through reference to a previous sentence.

Sentence sense lets us recognize the following:

1. That pronoun reference to a preceding sentence does not prevent a construction from being a sentence. Example:

SENTENCE: They showed it to us.

By itself, this sentence is far from having complete meaning, but it can stand alone.

2. That reference of a verb auxiliary to a preceding sentence does not prevent a construction from being a sentence. Example:

SENTENCE: I will if you can.

The auxiliaries *will* and *can* must draw their meaning from verbs in a preceding sentence. Still, in spite of its lack of meaning, this construction is a sentence.

3. That the reference of *so, thus, then,* and *there* to a preceding sentence does not prevent a construction from being a sentence. Example:

SENTENCE: So did Aunt Martha.

Both *so* and *did* must get their meaning from the preceding sentence.

4. That a construction may begin with a coordinating connective or transitional phrase and still stand alone as a sentence. Examples:

SENTENCES: But they didn't.
For example, the price of gasoline has gone up again.

Coordinating connectives and transitional phrases are frequently used to begin sentences, especially when the relationship with the preceding sentence is clear.

On the other hand, sentence sense lets us recognize the following:

1. That a clause beginning with a subordinating connective (subordinating conjunctions, relative pronouns, and a few connectives such as *that* and *what*) is **not** a sentence. Examples:

NONSENTENCES: Although Harry invited me to his apartment.
Because he wanted to show me his etchings.
What Howard actually said after I got there.

The subordinating connectives *although, because,* and *what* keep these meaningful subject-predicate combinations from being sentences.

2. That a construction without a subject and predicate is not a sentence. Examples:

NONSENTENCES: To sleep. Perhaps to dream.
Without a penny to my name.
Claiming to be a messenger from outer space.

Though these constructions deliver more meaning than, say, the sentence *he could,* they are not sentences because they do not have subject-predicate combinations.

If you find that you need to refer to this chapter or Chapter 3 very often, you need to work on developing your sentence sense. You should carefully study Sections 1B and 1D and perhaps all of Chapter 1.

2A DETACHED CLAUSES AS SENTENCE FRAGMENTS

Write in complete sentences; do not let a dependent clause stand as a sentence.

A common kind of sentence fragment is a **detached dependent clause** which, instead of standing by itself with a beginning capital letter and end punctuation, should be attached to the preceding sentence, sometimes with and sometimes without a comma separating it. Examples, with the fragments italicized:

WRONG: I didn't know what time it was. *Because my watch had lost its minute hand.*

RIGHT: I didn't know what time it was because my watch had lost its minute hand.

WRONG: It had come loose. *While I was chopping wood for our new woodstove.*

RIGHT: It had come loose while I was chopping wood for our new woodstove.

WRONG: We had bought one the week before. *Since we wanted to reduce our heating costs.*

RIGHT: We had bought one the week before, since we wanted to reduce our heating costs.

Subordinating connectives such as *because, since,* and *while* prevent detached dependent clauses from standing as sentences.

2B DETACHED PHRASES AS SENTENCE FRAGMENTS

Write in complete sentences; do not let a phrase stand as a sentence.

A construction without a subject-predicate combination— that is, a phrase rather than a clause—is a fragment even if it is not introduced by a subordinating connective. Such

detached phrases are a common source of sentence fragments. Examples, with the detached phrases italicized:

WRONG: Our heating costs remained the same. *Instead of going down.*
RIGHT: Our heating costs remained the same instead of going down.

WRONG: We invested in a used pickup. *To haul the wood.*
RIGHT: We invested in a used pickup to haul the wood.

WRONG: Dad also bought a new chain saw. *A gasoline model.*
RIGHT: Dad also bought a new chain saw, a gasoline model.

Noun, prepositional, and verbal phrases frequently are detached from the sentences they belong to, thus becoming sentence fragments. Detached clauses and phrases are usually due to the writer's lack of sentence sense.

2C SENTENCE FRAGMENTS DUE TO CONFUSED STRUCTURE

Write in complete sentences; avoid jumbled structures.

A third, but less common, kind of sentence fragment is one in which a necessary part of a sentence has been omitted or in which the sentence structure is jumbled rather than complete. Examples:

WRONG: Most homeowners who buy woodstoves to save on fuel costs, which is the main reason for making such a purchase.
RIGHT: Most homeowners who buy woodstoves to save on fuel costs, which is the main reason for making such a purchase, do not recover their investment for several years.

WRONG: People who should exercise extreme caution while using a chain saw, but they are sometimes careless.
RIGHT: People should exercise extreme caution while using a chain saw, but they are sometimes careless.

In the first example, the writer forgot to compose a predicate that would finish the sentence. In the second, the writer also forgot to provide a predicate for the subject *people* and instead let the sentence become a jumbled fragment. Such fragments are often due to the writer's carelessness.

2D   FRAGMENTS WITH NONFINITE VERB FORMS

Write in complete sentences; do not let a construction with a nonfinite verb form stand as a sentence.

A fourth, but not very common, type of sentence fragment is a construction with a **nonfinite verb form** rather than a finite (sentence-forming) verb form. Examples, with the nonfinite verb forms italicized:

WRONG: I did that once and then *going* to the doctor and *having* my wound stitched.

RIGHT: I did that once and then had to go to the doctor and have my wound stitched.

WRONG: That kind of foolishness *can making* the total cost quite high.

RIGHT: That kind of foolishness can make the total cost quite high.

Many, perhaps most, such fragments are due to carelessness, but some are due to the writer's lack of sentence sense.

3

Comma Splices and Run-Together Sentences

Independent clauses are in effect simple sentences, and two of them (perhaps with other constituents or sentence parts) are very often joined to form compound or compound-complex sentences. But when two independent clauses have *only* a comma and *no coordinating conjunction (and, but, yet, or, nor, so, for)* between them, a **comma splice** is formed, usually indicating that the writer has imperfect sentence sense. Without a coordinating conjunction between independent clauses, either a semicolon or a period between them is required. (A semicolon has the same force as a period, but is normally used only when the independent clauses are especially closely related.) If a period is the best mark of punctuation to use, then the second sentence of course begins with a capital letter.

3A COMMA SPLICES WITHOUT CONNECTIVE WORDS

Do not use a comma to separate two independent clauses that are not joined by a coordinating conjunction.

Many times a comma only, with no connective, is placed between sentences (or independent clauses), thus incorrectly "splicing" the sentences and producing a **comma splice.** In such cases, the second sentence usually begins with some kind of word—such as *this, another, there, it,* and other pronouns—that leads the writer to believe that the sentence is continuing, when actually a new sentence has begun. Either a period or, occasionally, a semicolon must replace the comma to eliminate the comma splice. Examples:

WRONG: Many times a homeowner wants to install another electrical outlet in a room, he needs an additional spot to plug in a lamp or a fan.

RIGHT: Many times a homeowner wants to install another electrical outlet in a room. He needs an additional spot to plug in a lamp or a fan.

WRONG: He first locates the stud behind the wall, then he cuts a small opening to receive the outlet box.

RIGHT: He first locates the stud behind the wall. Then he cuts a small opening to receive the outlet box.

WRONG: How can he drill a hole through the floor inside the wall, he needs a brace with an elbow.

RIGHT: How can he drill a hole through the floor inside the wall? He needs a brace with an elbow.

WRONG: Stringing the wires to the fuse box is not too hard, making the final connections is even easier.

RIGHT: Stringing the wires to the fuse box is not too hard; making the final connections is even easier.

In the last example a period instead of a semicolon would also be correct. A semicolon calls for the same duration of voice pause that a period does. Thus where a period at the end of a sentence is correct, a semicolon normally cannot be called wrong, though it may produce awkward style.

3B COMMA SPLICES WITH CONJUNCTIVE ADVERBS

Do not use a comma to separate two independent clauses joined by a conjunctive adverb.

The conjunctive adverbs like *however, therefore, nevertheless* are coordinating connectives frequently used to join sentences (or independent clauses), but they are not coordinating conjunctions. When a comma (instead of a period or semicolon) is used with them between sentences, a comma splice occurs. Example:

WRONG: The ordinary homeowner with minimal skills can probably do the job, however, he must have it inspected by a licensed electrician to conform to building codes.

RIGHT: The ordinary homeowner with minimal skills can probably do the job; however, he must have it inspected by a licensed electrician to conform to building codes.

Note several points here: (1) With a comma before and after *however,* the rapid reader might not at first know which clause the *however* goes with; quite often sentences end with a conjunctive adverb. (2) A period rather than a semicolon after *job* would also be correct. And (3) the *however* could be shifted to the interior of the second clause, for example, after *must* or after *electrician.* Most of the conjunctive adverbs can be shifted to the interior of the second clause, and this fact provides you with a test for proper punctuation: if the connective can be shifted, a period or semicolon must come after the first clause.

Another example:

WRONG: Building codes vary from one city to the next, therefore, a wise person will check them before he begins.
RIGHT: Building codes vary from one city to the next. Therefore, a wise person will check them before he begins.

A semicolon after *next* would not be wrong. The *therefore* could be shifted, as in *A wise person, therefore, will. . . .*

One more example:

WRONG: Plugging in the lamp caused our fuse to blow instantly,
then I decided to start from the beginning again.
RIGHT: Plugging in the lamp caused our fuse to blow instantly;
then I decided to start from the beginning again.

In this sentence *then* is a conjunctive adverb, not a coordinating conjunction; thus either a semicolon or a period must come after *instantly*. The *then* could be shifted to come after *decided,* but that structure might sound awkward. Nevertheless, that shift is a test that shows the necessity of a semicolon or period between the clauses.

3C   RUN-TOGETHER SENTENCES

Do not run two sentences together with no punctuation between them and no capital letter beginning the second sentence.

The error known as **run-together sentences** means that two sentences are run together with no punctuation or coordinating conjunction between them and no capital letter starting the second sentence. This error generally occurs when the second sentence starts with a word such as *this, another, there, it,* or some other pronoun, which sometimes leads the writer to believe he or she is continuing a sentence, not starting a new one. Examples:

WRONG: After the accident I decided to read the directions that
is what I should have done in the first place.
RIGHT: After the accident I decided to read the directions. That
is what I should have done in the first place.

WRONG: The second attempt worked perfectly this is what we had wanted all along.

RIGHT: The second attempt worked perfectly. This is what we had wanted all along.

In such run-together sentences the fact that the second sentence does not begin with a capital letter usually indicates that the writer has not been careless but lacks full sentence sense. Semicolons could be used instead of periods between such independent clauses, but periods are usually better.

If you find that you must refer to this chapter often, you probably need to study Sections 1B and 1D carefully and perhaps need to study all of Chapter 1.

4

Misused Modifiers

A **modifier** is a word or word group that describes, limits, or adds to another word or word group. Adjectives answer questions like *which one* and *what kind* about the noun. Adverbs answer questions like *when, where, why, how, how often,* and *under what circumstances* about the verb.

The common misuses of modifiers are the incorrect use of an adjective for an adverb to modify a verb and the incorrect use of an adverb as a predicate adjective.

4A MISUSED ADJECTIVE FORMS

Do not use an adjective form to modify an intransitive or transitive verb.

Such a misused adjective form almost always follows the verb it modifies. To determine whether a word is modifying a verb, remember that asking *what goes with what* is a useful test. For example, consider the following correct sentence:

Jack comes to our nightly big bashes very seldom.

Ask "What does *seldom* go with?" and your answer should be *seldom comes,* showing that *seldom* modifies (goes with) the verb of the sentence and is correctly used as an adverb.

Here are examples of adjectives misused for adverbs, with the modified verb underlined:

WRONG: When he called me by long distance, I had to speak each word *clear* and *distinct.*

RIGHT: When he called me by long distance, I had to speak each word **clearly** and **distinctly.**

WRONG: At first I was nervous on my first date, but he talked very *friendly* and that put me at ease.

RIGHT: At first I was nervous on my first date, but he talked **in a friendly way** and that put me at ease.

In the first example the *ly* adverb forms *clearly* and *distinctly* are needed to modify the verb *to speak.* In the second example *friendly* is one of a few adjectives (*heavenly, lovely,* and others) that end in *ly* but that almost never function as adverbs. Since the adverb form *friendlily* sounds awkward, the adverbial prepositional phrase *in a friendly way* is needed to modify the verb *talked.*

Three other examples:

WRONG: You explain it all so *clear* that I am learning more English than ever before.

RIGHT: You explain it all so **clearly** that I am learning more English than ever before.

WRONG: John had to weave in and out among the barricades real *careful* to avoid hitting them.

RIGHT: John had to weave in and out among the barricades quite **carefully** to avoid hitting them.

WRONG: After he became a rock star, Willie began <u>to</u> <u>dress</u>
        more colorful than before.
RIGHT: After he became a rock star, Willie began <u>to</u> <u>dress</u>
        more colorfully than before.

The adverb forms *clearly, carefully,* and *more colorfully*
are needed to modify the verbs *explain, to weave,* and
to dress.

A particularly sticky writing problem involves *well,*
which is both an adjective and an adverb, and *good,*
which is only an adjective. A writer should always use *well*
to modify a verb. Here are examples, with the verbs underlined:

WRONG: He <u>plays</u> the piano *good,* but he can't get a clear note
        out <u>of</u> a saxophone.
RIGHT: He <u>plays</u> the piano **well,** but he can't get a clear note
        out of a saxophone.

WRONG: I'm sure I <u>did</u> *good* on the final, but I still got only a C
        for the course.
RIGHT: I'm sure I <u>did</u> **well** on the final, but I still got only a C for
        the course.

The italicized words modify the verbs *plays* and *did,* and
thus the adverb *well,* not the adjective *good,* is required.
Remember that you *do well, write well, play well, argue
well, dress well, behave well,* and *work well.* (You can
feel good or *feel well,* with somewhat different meanings.)

Another adjective form sometimes misused for an
adverb is *near* for *nearly.* Examples:

WRONG: My paper wasn't *near* as bad as your red marks made
        it seem.
RIGHT: My paper wasn't **nearly** as bad as your red marks
        made it seem.

WRONG: But my father, in spite of what he said, wasn't *near* as
        mad as my mother.
RIGHT: But my father, in spite of what he said, wasn't **nearly** as
        mad as my mother.

Remember that the correct phrase is *not nearly as* . . . .

A related problem is the misuse of the noun *fun* as an adjective. Example:

WRONG: We had a *fun* time at the dance.
RIGHT: We had a **good** time at the dance.
OR:
RIGHT: We had **fun** at the dance. (*Fun* is now used correctly as a noun, not as an adjective modifying *time.*)

4B MISUSED ADVERB FORMS

Do not use an adverb to function as a predicate adjective after a linking verb.

After a linking verb, the correct modifier is not an adverb, but an adjective which describes the subject. The chief linking verbs are *to be, to get, to feel, to seem, to sound, to taste, to look, to remain, to become,* and *to appear.* Sometimes verbs that are normally linking—such as *to feel* and *to taste*—are used as intransitive or transitive verbs. Examples:

When she lost her wedding ring, Mother **felt** terrible. (LINKING)
When she wanted to make a new blouse, Mother **felt** the material first. (TRANSITIVE)

After a hard day in the woods, bean and bacon soup **tastes** good. (LINKING)
Before dinner was served, Dad always **tasted** the soup. (TRANSITIVE)

Occasionally certain intransitive or transitive verbs may function as linking verbs. The clue is that the linking verb is followed by an adjective that modifies the subject or by a predicate noun that renames the subject. Thus such verbs as *to go, to turn, to marry, to die,* and *to retire* are normally intransitive or transitive but occasionally function as linking, being followed by predicate adjectives that describe the subjects. Examples:

Orval went home. (INTRANSITIVE) The well went **dry.** (LINK-ING)

The burglar turned the key. (TRANSITIVE) Billy **turned** hostile. (LINKING)

Elsa married Howard. (TRANSITIVE) Louise married **young.** (LINKING)

Clarence died yesterday. (INTRANSITIVE) Dave died **old.** (LINKING)

Al retired two years ago. (INTRANSITIVE) Fred retired **happy.** (LINKING)

Since the meanings of each second example are *dry well, hostile Billy, young Louise, old Dave,* and *happy Fred,* the verbs in these instances are linking, and adjectives must follow them.

The most commonly misused adverb form is *badly* after the linking verb *to feel.* Examples:

WRONG: After I was caught plagiarizing, I felt very *badly.*
RIGHT: After I was caught plagiarizing, I felt very **bad.**

WRONG: When I began to see what grown-ups do, I didn't feel so *badly* about having shoplifted when I was in my early teens.
RIGHT: When I began to see what grown-ups do, I didn't feel so **bad** about having shoplifted when I was in my early teens.

WRONG: I felt *badly* when I realized how I had hurt my parents.
RIGHT: I felt **bad** when I realized how I had hurt my parents.

In these cases *feel* and *felt* are linking verbs, and therefore the adjective *bad* is needed as a predicate adjective to modify the subject *I.* Technically, *to feel badly* would mean to have a faulty sense of touch, such as being unable to tell whether a surface is smooth or rough. Also note that you would be very unlikely to say either of the following sentences:

WRONG: I feel *sadly* about your divorce.
WRONG: I feel *gladly* that you made an A.

Sad and *glad* are clearly the correct predicate adjective forms, as is *bad.*

Occasionally a writer will incorrectly use other adverb forms with linking verbs, probably because of having heard the incorrect *I feel badly* construction. Examples:

WRONG: Sleeping outside in the rain on our camping trip, we all felt as *miserably* as could be.

RIGHT: Sleeping outside in the rain on our camping trip, we all felt as **miserable** as could be.

WRONG: I remember how *horribly* Dad sounded when he found out I broke his best fishing rod.

RIGHT: I remember how **horrible** Dad sounded when he found out I broke his best fishing rod.

Miserable and *horrible* are needed as predicate adjectives to go with the linking verbs *felt* and *sounded* and to modify the subjects *we* and *Dad*. In the last example, the predicate adjective precedes its linking verb and subject. This is not an especially common construction but is not rare, either.

4C DOUBLE NEGATIVES

Do not use a double negative.

A **double negative** is a construction in which two words expressing negation—such as *not* and *nobody,* and *not* and *no*—are used to make one negative statement. In usage, such constructions are considered in the same unacceptable category as *ain't.* Examples, with the two negative words italicized:

WRONG: When I first got to St. Louis, I did*n't* know *nobody* but my cousin Hank.

RIGHT: When I first got to St. Louis, I did**n't** know **anybody** but my cousin Hank.

WRONG: It does*n't* do *no* good to complain; I've sent three letters already.

RIGHT: It does**n't** do **any** good to complain; I've sent three letters already.

Remember that the correct constructions are *not . . . any, not . . . anything, not . . . anyone,* and *don't (doesn't) . . . any* (rather than *no*).

Another incorrect double negative involves the words *hardly* and *scarcely.* Since these words are both negatives, using another negative in a construction with one of them produces a double negative. Examples, with the double negatives italicized:

WRONG: Her closets bulging, my daughter still complains that she does*n't* have *hardly* any clothes to wear.

RIGHT: Her closets bulging, my daughter still complains that she has **hardly any** clothes to wear.

WRONG: It was*n't scarcely* daybreak by the time we had saddled our horses.

RIGHT: It **was scarcely** daybreak by the time we had saddled our horses.

Remember never to use *no* or *not* in a construction with *hardly* or *scarcely.*

5

Pronoun Case Forms

Case is the grammatical function that requires (though not in all instances) the change of the form of a pronoun according to its use in a sentence. The **subjective case** forms like *I, we, she* are used as subjects and as predicate nouns, or, more exactly, predicate pronouns. The **objective case** forms like *me, us, her* are used as objects of verbs and prepositions. And the **possessive case** forms like *my, our, her* are used to show possession. Sometimes writers use incorrect pronoun case forms.

5A IN COMPOUND CONSTRUCTIONS

In compound constructions use subjective case forms as subjects and objective case forms as objects.

A compound construction is one in which two or more parts are coordinated, or used in a series of three or more. Very seldom does anyone use a wrong pronoun case form when a single pronoun is a subject or object. For example, you could wait for years and probably not hear such constructions as these:

WRONG: *Me* was invited to Jane's party.
WRONG: The package was for *I*.

But often when two pronouns, or a noun and a pronoun, occur in a compound construction, a faulty pronoun case form is used.

Here are examples in compound subjects, with the faulty pronoun forms italicized:

WRONG: George and *me* decided to go to the movies.
RIGHT: George and **I** decided to go to the movies.

WRONG: The mechanic and *him* fixed the transmission.
RIGHT: The mechanic and **he** fixed the transmission.

The subjective forms *I* and *he* are needed to serve as subjects of *decided* and *fixed*. When in doubt you can test such constructions by omitting one part of the compound construction. That is, omit *George* and *the mechanic* in the above examples and you will immediately see that *me decided to go to the movies* and *him fixed the transmission* are incorrect. Remember that the correct expressions are those such as these: *Melissa and she arrived, José and I conferred, the Joneses and they are . . ., the Alvarados and we began . . . .*

Similarly, subjective case forms should *not* be used in compound constructions that are objects of verbs or prepositions. Examples, with the incorrect pronoun case form italicized:

WRONG: My aunt asked my sister and *I* if we would help care for her lawn.
RIGHT: My aunt asked my sister and **me** if we would help care for her lawn.

WRONG: Between Jody and *I*, we thought it was a good way to earn some money.
RIGHT: Between Jody and **me,** we thought it was a good way to earn some money.

Again, a simple test is to drop one part of the compound structure. You would not write "My aunt asked I . . ." or "Between I . . . ." Clearly, since the pronoun is the object of the verb *asked* and of the preposition *between,* the objective form—*me*—is needed. Remember that the correct expressions are those such as these: *between you and me, for Tom and him, with Jack and me, overheard Mary and her, invited the Medinas and us.*

5B AFTER *TO BE*

Use subjective pronoun forms after forms of the verb *to be.*

Since the verb *to be* is a linking verb, any predicate noun or pronoun that follows a form of it renames the subject. Therefore since the subject is, obviously, in the subjective case, a predicate pronoun, which is the same as the subject, should also be in the subjective case. But in informal use nowadays, especially in speech, objective pronoun forms are usually acceptable after forms of *to be.* Examples, with the pronouns in boldface:

INFORMAL: It's **me.**
INFORMAL: I'm sure it was **her.**
INFORMAL: Could you have been **him?**
INFORMAL: Did you think it was **us?**

However, in semiformal and formal situations subjective pronoun case forms should follow forms of *to be.* Examples:

SEMIFORMAL: It's **I.**
SEMIFORMAL: The guilty ones were **they.**
SEMIFORMAL: I'm sure it was **she.**
SEMIFORMAL: It might be **he** who wins.

Even in informal conversation many people still prefer the subjective case forms in such constructions.

5C WHO AND WHOM

Use *who* (or *whoever*) in subject positions and *whom* (or *whomever*) in object positions.

However, it is customary nowadays in informal conversation to use *who* as an object except directly after a preposition. Examples:

INFORMAL: **Who** did you vote for? (object of *vote for*)
INFORMAL: I told you **who** you should call. (object of *call*)

But in semiformal or formal writing you should distinguish between *who* and *whom.* Examples:

RIGHT: I explained the problem to the clerk **whom** I was talking to. (object of *talking to*)
RIGHT: Then the clerk referred me to the manager, **who,** she said, would correct the error. (subject of *would correct*)
RIGHT: After his failure, I was ready to turn to **whoever** could help me. (subject of *could help*)

Sometimes you may need to test a construction in order to choose the right form of *who.* The test is this: (1) turn a question into a simple sentence or express the part of a sentence containing a form of *who* as a simple sentence; then (2) see whether *he* or *him* fits the *who* slot in your simple sentence. If *he* fits, use *who;* if *him* fits, use *whom.* Examples:

_____ did you see at the game?
(Who *or* Whom?)

You saw *him* at the game. (not *he*)
Whom did you see at the game?

_____ did you say brought Charlotte?
(Who *or* Whom?)

You did say *he* brought Charlotte. (not *him*)
Who did you say brought Charlotte?

We usually avoid someone _____ we owe
money to.   (who *or* whom?)

We owe money to *him.* (So use *whom* as the object of *to,*
even though *whom* doesn't come directly after *to.*)
We usually avoid someone **whom** we owe money to.

Keith is the person _____ it seems will be
                            (who *or* whom?)
chosen homecoming king.

It seems *he* will be chosen. (So use *who* as the subject of *will
be chosen.*)
Keith is the person **who** it seems will be chosen homecoming king.

The test is simple and reliable. We should note that even
in casual conversation some people still prefer to distinguish between *who* and *whom.*

5D IN COMPARATIVE CONSTRUCTIONS

**After the comparative words *as* and *than* use the pro-
noun case form that the understood part of the clause
calls for.**

In such a sentence as

I gave more to charity than _____,
                               (he *or* him?)

a part of a dependent clause is understood but not stated.
In the above sentence the understood part is *(than he)
gave to charity.* Testing such sentences by mentally supplying the understood part of the clause will tell you the
correct pronoun to use. Examples, with the understood
parts in parentheses:

RIGHT: My sister was married earlier than **I** (was married).
RIGHT: Father's will left her as much inheritance as (it left) **me.**

RIGHT: The coach gave the other team members as much credit as (he gave) **me.**

RIGHT: The coach gave the other team members as much credit as **I** (gave them credit).

As the last two examples show, the pronoun form at the end of a comparative construction sometimes determines the meaning. The test for choosing the correct form is both simple and reliable.

5E   WITH VERBAL PHRASES

Use the possessive form of a pronoun (or noun) to modify an *ing* verbal phrase when the phrase refers to just one aspect of a person and not the person as a whole.

Example, with the pronoun form in boldface:

RIGHT: We all agreed with Derick, but we could see that the coach was furious at **his** not having followed orders.

Him would be incorrect, for the coach was not furious at him as a whole but only at his not having followed orders. Two more examples:

RIGHT: Jill heard **me** coming, and she did not like **my** coming on a motorcycle.

RIGHT: We were delayed by the **McCombs'** arriving an hour late.

The *me* is correct because it refers to the whole person, and the *my* is correct because it refers to just one action of the person. In other words, the sentence does not say that "she did not like me" but only that she did not like one of my actions. Similarly, the possessive form *McCombs'* is correct: we were delayed by an action of *theirs,* not by the McCombs themselves.

5F THE *WE STUDENTS-US STUDENTS* CONSTRUCTION

Use *we* or *us* in conjunction with a noun according to whether the noun functions as a subject or object.

If the noun is a subject, use *we;* if it is an object, use *us.* The very simple test that will guide you correctly in choosing *we* or *us* is to mentally omit the noun and then to use the pronoun form that sounds natural. Examples, with the noun to be mentally omitted in parentheses:

RIGHT: After failing to persuade the dean, **we** (freshmen) took our case directly to the president.

RIGHT: The president treated **us** (students) with dignity and patience.

RIGHT: Some people imagine that **we** (girls) in the sororities don't study as hard as those in the dorms.

RIGHT: The board chairman made it clear to **us** (stockholders) why our dividends were so low this year.

Since no one would write such constructions as *us took* or *to we,* this simple test is thoroughly reliable.

5G DEMONSTRATIVE PRONOUNS

Never use *them* as a demonstrative ("pointing") pronoun in place of *these* or *those.*

Examples:

WRONG: I asked for *them* books to be reserved for me.
RIGHT: I asked for **those** books to be reserved for me.

WRONG (pointing and speaking with emphasis): I want one of *them.*
RIGHT: I want one of **those** (or **these**).

When there is no pointing action, *them* is correct, as in the following sentence:

I was the first to see **them.**

5H REFLEXIVE PRONOUNS

In semiformal or formal writing do not use a reflexive pronoun as a subject or object.

Examples:

WRONG: Jerry and *myself* managed to slip through the transom into our dorm's kitchen.

RIGHT: Jerry and **I** managed to slip through the transom into our dorm's kitchen.

WRONG: It turned out that the invitation was for both my brother and *myself.*

RIGHT: It turned out that the invitation was for both my brother and **me.**

Use the reflexive pronoun as an object only when it refers to the same person as the subject, as in *I cut myself.*

Also avoid these incorrect spellings of the reflexive pronouns: *hisself, theirselves,* and *its self.* The correct forms are *himself, themselves,* and *itself.*

6

Subject-Verb Agreement

The grammatical term **number** has to do, obviously, with the number of units involved. The two numbers in our grammar are the **singular** (one) and the **plural** (more than one). For writing to be correct, verbs must agree in number with their subjects.

Most English nouns and pronouns show singular and plural number by a change in form.

Singular	Plural
car	cars
boat	boats
peach	peaches
man	men
I	we
you	you
he, she, it	they

All English verbs except one show a distinct number only in the present tense. When *he, she,* or *it* (or an expression that can replace these pronouns) is the subject, *s* or *es* is added to the stem of the verb. In the following examples, consider only the verbs themselves.

I eat	we eat	I touch	we touch
you eat	you eat	you touch	you touch
he eat**s**	they eat	he touch**es**	they touch

I do	we do	I have	we have
you do	you do	you have	you have
he do**es**	they do	he ha**s**	they have

The irregular verb *to be* shows number in both the present and past tenses.

Present		*Past*	
I **am**	we **are**	I **was**	we **were**
you **are**	you **are**	you **were**	you **were**
he **is**	they **are**	he **was**	they **were**

Modal auxiliaries (page 17) do not change at all. The same form is used whether the subject is singular or plural.

I **can** run	we **must** hurry
you **may** eat	you **shall** perish
he **will** show	they **ought to** behave

Although there are limited opportunities to make errors in subject-verb agreement in English, there still are a number of trouble spots, and we will cover them in the following sections.

6A NOUN PHRASES AS SUBJECTS

The verb of a sentence should agree in number with the headword of a noun-phrase subject.

Of course, many subjects are single nouns, such as a person's name. But often a noun phrase functions as a subject. The whole noun phrase is the **full subject,** and the **headword** of the noun phrase is the **simple subject.** The headword is the noun (or noun substitute, such as *many*) that governs the entire phrase; all other words and word groups in the noun phrase either modify the headword or modify other words in the phrase. The simple subject, or headword of the noun phrase, governs the verb. Thus singular headwords call for singular verbs and plural headwords call for plural verbs. Here are examples, with the headwords, or simple subjects, and the verbs in boldface:

RIGHT: A professional **man** from the Twin Cities **visits** us regularly.
RIGHT: The **car** with two wheels missing **was** our secret hideout.

The singular headwords (simple subjects) *man* and *car* govern the singular verbs *visits* and *was.*

RIGHT: Several **coeds** with no brains but lots of money **were** very popular in Las Vegas.

The plural simple subject *coeds* takes the plural verb *were.*

When the headword is followed by a prepositional phrase with the compound preposition *as well as* or *together with,* the object of the prepositional phrase does not affect the verb. Also, the prepositional phrase is often set off by commas. Examples:

WRONG: The *scoutmaster,* as well as the advanced scouts, *were* trying to bully us tenderfeet.
RIGHT: The **scoutmaster,** as well as the advanced scouts, **was** trying to bully us tenderfeet.

WRONG: The *babysitter,* together with the three children, *were* rescued from the blazing apartment.
RIGHT: The **babysitter,** together with the three children, **was** rescued from the blazing apartment.

6B INDEFINITE PRONOUNS AS SUBJECTS

The indefinite pronouns *one, each, either,* and *neither* are singular and require singular verbs.

Examples:

WRONG: *Either* of the recipes *make* good pies.
RIGHT: **Either** of the recipes **makes** good pies.

RIGHT: Only **one** of the recipes **requires** real butter.
RIGHT: **Neither takes** longer than thirty-five minutes.
RIGHT: **Each** of the pies **serves** six easily.

The indefinite pronouns *any* and *none* may correctly take either a singular or a plural verb. Example:

RIGHT: **None** of you **are** (or **is**) to blame.
RIGHT: **Any** of the voters **is** (or **are**) entitled to challenge the candidates.

6C RELATIVE PRONOUNS AS SUBJECTS

When a relative pronoun functions as a subject, its verb agrees in number with the pronoun's antecedent.

This means that *who, which,* and *that* are either singular or plural according to the nouns they refer to. Examples, with the relative pronoun, its antecedent, and the verb in boldface:

RIGHT: I have an **uncle** in Peoria **who** still **makes** bathtub gin.
RIGHT: The **theories** of cosmogony **which** in the future **are** likely to be re-examined are the big-bang and steady-state theories.

A special subject-verb agreement problem involving relative pronouns appears in sentences with the construction *one of those _____ who* (or *which* or *that*). Example:

RIGHT: Jean-Paul is one of those Frenchmen who eat snails.
(*Eats* would be wrong.)

The point is that *Frenchmen,* and not *Jean-Paul,* is the antecedent of *who,* which means that a plural verb is required. When in doubt, you can use a simple test to choose the proper verb. All such sentences as the one illustrated will undergo this transformation:

Of those **Frenchmen who eat** snails, Jean-Paul is one.

This test clearly shows the verb form needed.

6D COMPOUND SUBJECTS

Compound subjects consist of two or more coordinated constituents (or unified parts of a sentence).

6D1 With the Coordinating Conjunction *and*

When two (or more) subjects are joined by *and*, they form a plural subject and should take a plural verb.

Examples:

RIGHT: My uncle **and** one of my cousins **are** going to Las Vegas with me.

RIGHT: Where you go **and** whom you go with **are** none of my business.

But when two nouns or constructions joined by *and* are considered a single unit, they take a singular verb. Examples:

RIGHT: Peaches and cream **is** my favorite dessert.

RIGHT: When Billy makes a sandwich, the peanut butter and jelly always **oozes** out the side.

Peaches and cream is considered a single dish, and the combination of *peanut butter and jelly* is treated as a single unit.

6D2 With Correlatives and *but not*

When compound subjects are joined by one of the correlatives or by *but not,* the verb agrees in number with the part of the subject closer to the verb.

The correlatives are the two-part connectives *either (neither) . . . or (nor), not only . . . but (also),* and *not . . . but.* (The correlative *both . . . and* makes compound subjects just as *and* by itself does.) Examples, with the noun governing the verb and the verb in boldface:

RIGHT: Neither the payments nor the **interest was** exorbitant.
RIGHT: Neither the interest nor the **payments were** exorbitant.

RIGHT: Not only the son but also the **daughters were** invited.
RIGHT: Not only the daughters but also the **son was** invited.

RIGHT: Either two tablets or one **spoonful is** recommended.
RIGHT: Either one spoonful or two **tablets are** recommended.

Sometimes the *either* of *either . . . or* and the *also* of *not only . . . but also* are omitted, but the rule for subject-verb agreement stays the same.
     When two subjects are joined by the connective *but not,* the verb agrees in number with the part of the subject closer to the verb. Examples:

RIGHT: All the wives but not a single **husband was** willing to go.
RIGHT: Mr. Busbee but not his **children were** willing to go.

6E SPECIAL NOUNS AS SUBJECTS

Three special kinds of nouns sometimes cause problems in subject-verb agreement.

6E1 Collective Nouns

Collective nouns take singular verbs unless they are used so as to mean individuals and not a group.

Collective nouns are those singular in form but plural in meaning, since they specify many individuals. Some of the most common collective nouns are *family, team, crew, series, jury, flock, student body, faculty, staff, pride* (of lions), *gaggle* (of geese), and *collection.* Examples:

RIGHT: The **team is** scheduled to practice at 4:00.
RIGHT: The **student body meets** monthly.
RIGHT: The **series** of lectures beginning tomorrow **deals** with winemaking.

When a collective noun is used so that it must be thought of as meaning separate individuals, it takes a plural verb. Example:

RIGHT: My family **are** individualists.

Such use of collective nouns is not common.

The collective nouns *number, crowd, group,* and perhaps a few others pose a different problem. When one of these singular nouns is followed by a prepositional phrase with a plural noun object, the verb may be plural. Examples, with the simple subjects and the verbs in boldface:

RIGHT: A **number** of demonstrators **were** arrested.
RIGHT: A **crowd** of spectators **were** turned away.
RIGHT: A **group** of children **were** ushered into the concert hall.

Some writers prefer singular verbs in such sentences, and that usage is of course correct. But individuals are so clearly meant in the example sentences and others like them that the plural verb must also be considered correct. Some experts prefer the plural verb.

6E2 Singular Nouns Plural in Form

Normally, nouns plural in form but singular in meaning take singular verbs.

The most common such nouns are *economics, physics, mathematics, politics, statistics, checkers, measles, mumps,* and *molasses.* Examples:

RIGHT: Statistics **enables** one to lie with figures.
RIGHT: Mumps sometimes **affects** men adversely.
RIGHT: Physics **includes** the laws of energy and matter.

6E3 Nouns of Weight, Measurement, Time, and Money

A plural noun that establishes a weight or measurement or a period of time or an amount of money takes a singular verb.

Examples:

RIGHT: Seventy-two inches **equals** six feet.
RIGHT: Two hundred fifty miles **is** a short trip on a DC-10.
RIGHT: Ten days to two weeks **is** the usual length of time people suffer from the common cold.
RIGHT: Six hundred dollars **is** the best I can offer for that china closet.

6F SUBJECTS IN INVERTED SENTENCE ORDER

When a subject follows its verb, the verb still agrees in number with the subject.

Examples, with the verbs and subjects in boldface:

RIGHT: Sitting by his side **were** his wife and two sons.
RIGHT: Next to his feet **was** his Great Dane.

Note that the nouns *side* and *feet* have no effect on the verbs. The subjects are *his wife and two sons* and *his Great Dane.*

The most common kind of inverted sentence order, however, and the one that gives most trouble in subject-verb agreement, is the sentence that begins with *there* and has its subject following the verb. The *there* is just a filler and has no meaning. To find the real subject, rearrange the sentence by asking *who* or *what* of the verb.

Examples:

WRONG: There *has been* some good *programs* on public tele-vison. (THINK: Some good programs have been . . . .)

RIGHT: There **have been** some good **programs** on public tele-vision.

WRONG: There *exists* many *ways* for students to cheat on exams. (THINK: Many ways exist . . . .)

RIGHT: There **exist** many **ways** for students to cheat on exams.

When the opening word *there* does not mean a place, the sentence subject will follow its verb.

7

Shifts

Various kinds of inconsistencies frequently occur in writing because of **faulty shifts in grammatical constructions.** That is, a writer will begin with one kind of grammatical construction but will then unnecessarily (and incorrectly shift to a different kind of construction. Example:

INCONSISTENT: The American child is different from his European counterparts.

This writer opened with the singular *American child,* thus committing himself (or herself) to talking about children in general in the singular, which is perfectly acceptable. But then he inconsistently shifted to the plural *European counterparts.* The writer either should have continued in the singular with *European counterpart* or should have begun with the plural *American children.* Maintaining complete grammatical consistency is not an easy task even for professional writers. In this chapter we will deal briefly and simply with the six kinds of shifts that produce most inconsistencies. These are shifts in **number, person, tense, voice, mood,** and **point of view.**

7A IN NUMBER

Do not inconsistently shift from the singular to the plural or from the plural to the singular.

The most common kind of faulty shift in number is from a singular noun to a plural pronoun. Examples:

INCONSISTENT: A *person* may say that *they are* happy, but sometimes *they are* merely fooling *themselves*.
CONSISTENT: **People** may say that **they are** happy, but sometimes **they are** merely fooling **themselves.**

INCONSISTENT: If you send *them* a coupon, *a company* may offer you a bargain, but then *they take* three months before *they send* the item.
CONSISTENT: If you send **them** a coupon, certain **companies** may offer you a bargain, but then **they take** three months before **they send** the item.

Sometimes, however, the faulty shift is from the plural to the singular. Example:

INCONSISTENT: What *they* don't know won't hurt *a person.*
CONSISTENT: What **they** don't know won't hurt **them.**
OR:
CONSISTENT: What **a person** doesn't know won't hurt **him.**

You must give thought to whether you will write in the singular or the plural in order to avoid such shifts.

7B IN PERSON

Do not inconsistently shift from the third person to the second or from the second person to the third.

There are three **persons** in English grammar: (1) the **first person** is the person speaking *(I, me, we, us);* (2) the **second person** is the person spoken to *(you);* and (3) the **third person** is the person or thing spoken about (*he, him, she, her, it, they, them,* and all nouns and indefinite pronouns). The grammatical inconsistency dealt with in this section is due to our language's use of the **indefinite second person,** using *you* to refer to people in general. The indefinite *you* is not at all improper, but it is improper to begin a passage in the third person and then to shift inconsistently to the indefinite *you.* Examples:

INCONSISTENT: College is designed to aid *those* interested in becoming educated. Without the opportunity to attend college, *you* might not receive the education *you* will need in *your* vocation.

CONSISTENT: College is designed to aid **those** interested in becoming educated. Without the opportunity to attend college, **people** might not receive the education **they** will need in **their vocations.**

INCONSISTENT: *One* needs to know that *you* are loved.
CONSISTENT: **One** needs to know that **one** is loved.
OR:
CONSISTENT: **People** need to know that **they** are loved.

In the second example note the shift from *one* (the indefinite third person pronoun referring to people in general) to *you* (the second person pronoun). The first correction maintains consistency, but some would consider it poor style. The second correction shows consistency by using both the noun and the pronoun in the third person.

7C IN TENSE

In summarizing fiction or history, do not inconsistently shift from the past to the present tense or the present to the past tense.

There are a number of different present and past tenses, but we need not differentiate among them; just recognizing that a verb is in one of the present or one of the past tenses is enough. In summarizing events of the past we may use either the past tense or the **historical present tense,** but the writer who inconsistently shifts from one to the other is careless. Examples:

INCONSISTENT: In this movie a cowboy *came* to a small town. He *stops* at the local saloon and *finds* that a seething unrest *lies* hidden just below the outward calm.

CONSISTENT: In this movie a cowboy **comes** to a small town. He **stops** at the local saloon and **finds** that a seething unrest **lies** hidden just below the outward calm.

INCONSISTENT: In the 1932 election campaign FDR *promised* to reduce taxes if he was elected. But in 1933 he *begins* to ask Congress for tax increases and *continues* to ask for increases every year.

CONSISTENT: In the 1932 election campaign FDR **promised** to reduce taxes if he **was elected.** But in 1933 he **began** to ask Congress for tax increases and **continued** to ask for them every year.

In each of these examples the writer began a summary in the past tense and inconsistently shifted to the historical present. In the first example we restored consistency by changing the past tense *(came)* to the present *(comes).* In the second, we changed the present tense *(begins, continues)* to the past *(began, continued).* The point is to be consistent. You should *know* which tense you have chosen for a summary and should stick to it.

7D   IN VOICE

Do not inconsistently shift from the active to the passive voice.

In the active voice, the subject performs the action; in the passive voice the subject receives the action. Mature writers find the active voice more forceful, but there are on occasion good reasons for using the passive. However, once you have started describing a sequence of actions in the active voice, do not inconsistently shift to the passive. (If you shift from the passive to the active, you should have started in the active voice to begin with.) Example:

INCONSISTENT: I first *brought* two quarts of water to a boil. Next the frozen package *was dropped in.* After five minutes I *cut open* the plastic and *poured* the peas into a bowl.

CONSISTENT: I first **brought** two quarts of water to a boil. Next I **dropped in** the frozen package. After five minutes I **cut open** the plastic and **poured** the peas into a bowl.

In the inconsistent passage, the first and third sentences are properly in the active voice, but the middle sentence is inconsistently in the passive voice. Since the writer is performing all the actions, there is no reason to say vaguely that they are performed.

7E IN MOOD

Do not inconsistently shift from the imperative to the subjunctive mood.

Verbs have mood. Request or command sentences are in the imperative mood, which is also often used for giving directions. That is, you might say the following to someone:

First **go** to . . . . Then **take** the first left . . . . After that, **turn** at . . . .

The boldface verbs are in the imperative mood, directly telling someone to do certain things. One form of the subjunctive mood uses the modal auxiliaries *should* and *ought to* so that the writer does not tell someone to do something but rather that he or she *should* do something. In giving directions, do not inconsistently shift from the imperative to the subjunctive mood. Example:

INCONSISTENT: When you begin working on your kit, first *lay* out all the parts and *check* each one against the list. *Place* the items into different cups of a muffin tin or an egg carton. *You* should, of course, *have* your tools ready. Next, *you should read* the instruction manual. *Do* each step in order and *make* a check mark when you have completed it.

CONSISTENT: (Simply remove the *you should*'s from sentences three and four.)

It is possible, of course, to give directions so that *essential* steps are phrased in the imperative mood and *desirable* (but not essential) steps are phrased in the subjunctive mood, but no such differentiation exists in the passage above. To be consistent, such a passage requires that *lay, place, have, read,* and all the verbs be in the imperative mood.

7F IN POINT OF VIEW

Do not inconsistently shift the point of view when discussing or explaining someone's opinions.

Point of view refers to the source of an opinion or idea being presented. The writing should make clear whether the opinion is the writer's own or that of someone being discussed. Sentences should be composed so that the point of view does not inconsistently shift. Example:

INCONSISTENT: Everybody nowadays thinks slavery is a wholly inhumane and unacceptable institution, but Aristotle thought it was rooted in human nature and thus acceptable. Some people are born to be leaders and some to be followers or servants. Human nature can't be changed, and thus the slave class remains the slave class. Slavery is fixed in human nature.

CONSISTENT: Everybody nowadays thinks slavery is a wholly inhumane and unacceptable institution, but Aristotle thought that it was rooted in human nature and thus acceptable. **He claimed** that some people are born to be leaders and some to be followers or servants. **He maintained** that human nature can't be changed and that that is why the slave class remains the slave class. Slavery, **he argued,** is fixed in human nature.

In the inconsistent passage the writer begins by stating a modern point of view and contrasting it with Aristotle's. But it is unclear whether the last three sentences reflect what Aristotle thought or what people nowadays believe. In the consistent passage, the *he claimed, he maintained,* and *he argued* clearly retain Aristotle's point of view and prevent inconsistency.

8

Verb Forms

Incorrect subject-verb agreement (Chapter 6) perhaps accounts for most verb problems in writing. However, occasionally wrong verb forms are used, chiefly because English has both regular and irregular verbs that sometimes cause confusion. All English verbs (with slight exceptions for *to be*) have five forms, as follows:

infinitive	third-person singular, present tense	past tense	present participle	past participle
to talk	talks	talked	talking	talked
to freeze	freezes	froze	freezing	frozen
to bring	brings	brought	bringing	brought

The present tense (except for the third person) is always the infinitive without the *to.* Two of the remaining forms are always regular. The third-person singular present tense *always* ends in *s* or *es,* and the present participle of all verbs ends in *ing.* Differences in some verbs appear in the last two forms. Verbs that end in *ed* in the past tense and past participle are called **regular;** others are **irregular,** sometimes with the past tense and past participle being different from each other (as with *freeze*) and sometimes identical (as with *bring*).

For your reference, here is a list of the so-called **principal parts** of the chief irregular verbs in English. The stem is the present tense, or the infinitive without the *to*.

stem	*past tense*	*past participle*
arise	arose	has arisen
bear	bore	has borne, was born
begin	began	has begun
bind	bound	has bound
blow	blew	has blown
break	broke	has broken
bring	brought	has brought
buy	bought	has bought
catch	caught	has caught
choose	chose	has chosen
come	came	has come
creep	crept	has crept
deal	dealt	has dealt
dive	dived, dove	has dived
do	did	has done
draw	drew	has drawn
drink	drank	has drunk
drive	drove	has driven
eat	ate	has eaten
fall	fell	has fallen
flee	fled	has fled
fly	flew	has flown
forbid	forbad, forbade	has forbidden
freeze	froze	has frozen
give	gave	has given
go	went	has gone
grow	grew	has grown

stem	past tense	past participle
hang	hung	has hung
hang (execution)	hanged	has hanged
know	knew	has known
lay	laid	has laid
lead	led	has led
lie	lay	has lain
lose	lost	has lost
mean	meant	has meant
ride	rode	has ridden
ring	rang	has rung
rise	rose	has risen
run	ran	has run
see	saw	has seen
seek	sought	has sought
send	sent	has sent
shake	shook	has shaken
shine	shone, shined	has shown, has shined
sing	sang	has sung
sleep	slept	has slept
speak	spoke	has spoken
spin	spun	has spun
spit	spit, spat	has spit, has spat
spread	spread	has spread
steal	stole	has stolen
stink	stank	has stunk
swear	swore	has sworn
swim	swam	has swum
swing	swung	has swung
take	took	has taken
teach	taught	has taught
tear	tore	has torn
thrive	thrived, throve	has thrived, thriven
throw	threw	has thrown
wear	wore	has worn
weep	wept	has wept
write	wrote	has written

8A PAST-TENSE FORMS

Do not use the past participle of an irregular verb as the past-tense form, unless the two are identical.

Examples:

WRONG: Hank *run* the tractor without oil until he *seen* the smoke pouring out.

RIGHT: Hank **ran** the tractor without oil until he **saw** the smoke pouring out.

WRONG: The eggs left in the picnic basket from last summer sure *stunk.*

RIGHT: The eggs left in the picnic basket from last summer sure **stank.**

WRONG: I *swum* forty laps in record time.

RIGHT: I **swam** forty laps in record time.

8B PAST-PARTICIPLE FORMS; *COULD OF*

Do not use the past-tense form of an irregular verb as the past participle, unless the two are identical.

The past participle is always used with an auxiliary, often *has, have,* or *had* (see list above). Be particularly cautious when a form of *have* is contracted, as in *I've, he's,* or *they've.* Examples:

WRONG: *Have* you *did* your reading for tomorrow yet?

RIGHT: **Have** you **done** your reading for tomorrow yet?

WRONG: *We've went* 600 miles since this morning, and Harry *has drove* almost all the way.

RIGHT: **We've gone** 600 miles since this morning, and Harry **has driven** almost all the way.

WRONG: Willie *has rode* that old nag in every race and *has* never *rang* the victory bell once.

RIGHT: Willie **has ridden** that old nag in every race and **has** never **rung** the victory bell once.

Also, do not convert an irregular verb form into an incorrect regular form.

Examples:

WRONG: I really got excited when he *dealed* me three aces.
RIGHT: I really got excited when he **dealt** me three aces.

WRONG: His manager *throwed* in the towel after Eddie was *layed* out cold by that right cross.
RIGHT: His manager **threw** in the towel after Eddie was **laid** out by that right cross.

Never use the word *of* for the contraction of *have.*

The two forms sound the same in ordinary speech, and thus the error is common. Example:

WRONG: I *could of* made the team if I had tried harder.
RIGHT: I **could've (could have)** made the team if I had tried harder.

8C *TO LIE–TO LAY; TO SIT–TO SET; TO BEAR*

Do not confuse *lay* with *lie* or *set* with *sit*.

Here are the principal parts of these verbs.

present tense	present participle	past tense	past participle
lie, lies (to recline)	lying	lay	lain
lay, lays (to place or put)	laying	laid	laid
sit, sits (to be seated)	sitting	sat	sat
set, sets (to place something)	setting	set	set

To lie is an intransitive verb; virtually no one ever uses it incorrectly, that is, as a transitive verb (as in the incorrect *I will lie the book down*). Examples of its use:

RIGHT: I **lie** down when I have a headache.
RIGHT: I **lay** on the floor for hours before anyone found me.
RIGHT: I **had lain** in bed longer than usual.
RIGHT: I **had been lying** in the muck for some time.

To *lay* is a transitive verb and is used correctly only when it has a direct object. Examples, with the verbs and direct objects in boldface:

RIGHT: I **lay** my **gun** down whenever I hear other hunters.
RIGHT: I **laid** the **bottle** of wine slightly upended.
RIGHT: I **have laid** expensive **carpet** professionally for a year.
RIGHT: I **was laying** the **baby** down when the phone rang.

The errors come when forms of *lay* are used instead of forms of *lie.* In the following examples, *down, on the beach,* and *in bed* are not objects; they are adverbial modifiers. Hence, the intransitive verb *lie* is necessary, Examples:

WRONG: Let's *lay* down awhile before we climb the next hill.
RIGHT: Let's **lie** down awhile before we climb the next hill.

WRONG: That girl *has been laying* on the beach all morning.
RIGHT: That girl **has been lying** on the beach all morning.

WRONG: After his operation Dad *laid* in bed for ten days.
RIGHT: After his operation Dad **lay** in bed for ten days.

To *sit* is also an intransitive verb. Virtually no one ever uses it incorrectly, that is, as a transitive verb (as in the incorrect *I'll sit the table*). Examples of its use:

RIGHT: That empty bottle **sits** on the mantel as a symbol.
RIGHT: Another bottle **sat** there last year.
RIGHT: I **have sat** on antique chairs before.
RIGHT: Joe **has been sitting** in front of the TV for twelve hours.

To *set* is a transitive verb used correctly (except for some uncommon meanings) only when it has a direct object. Examples, with the verbs and direct objects in boldface:

RIGHT: I **will set** the **bottle** down immediately.
RIGHT: Yesterday I **set it** in a hiding place.
RIGHT: I **have set** potted **plants** all around the house.
RIGHT: I **was setting** the **plants** in their tubs when Mavis arrived.

The errors come when forms of *set* are used instead of forms of *sit*. Examples:

WRONG: I'd feel better if I could just *set* awhile.
RIGHT: I'd feel better if I could just **sit** awhile.

WRONG: The dog just *set* there and waited for my command.
RIGHT: The dog just **sat** there and waited for my command.

WRONG: He would have *set* there all day if I hadn't whistled.
RIGHT: He would have **sat** there all day if I hadn't whistled.

WRONG: We *were* just *setting* around talking.
RIGHT: We **were** just **sitting** around talking.

The verb *to bear* also needs mentioning. In active-voice sentences, its past participle is *borne.* Examples:

RIGHT: Elaine **has borne** six children.
RIGHT: I **have borne** all the slander I can take.

But in the passive voice, *born* is the past participle of *to bear* in the meaning of coming into the world. Example:

RIGHT: I **was born** in Muncie, Indiana.

8D SUBJUNCTIVE VERB FORMS

Do not use the indicative form of a verb when a subjunctive form is needed.

The subjunctive forms of all verbs but one differ from the indicative in only one way: there is no *s* on the third-person singular present tense. The verb *to be,* however, has distinct subjunctive forms in both tenses.

Present		*Past*	
(if) I be	(if) we be	(if) I were	(if) we were
(if) you be	(if) you be	(if) you were	(if) you were
(if) he be	(if) they be	(if) he were	(if) they were

The indicative mood states a fact or what is thought to be a fact. The subjunctive mood expresses a wish or a condition contrary to fact or it appears in a *that*-clause of resolution, recommendation, or demand. Examples:

WRONG: If only I *was* a rich man!
RIGHT: If only I **were** a rich man!

WRONG: It is necessary that each voter *registers.*
RIGHT: It is necessary that each voter **register.**

WRONG: I move that our visitor *is* permitted to speak on this matter.
RIGHT: I move that our visitor **be** permitted to speak on this matter.

SECTION TWO

PUNCTUATION AND MECHANICS

End Punctuation

End punctuation occurs at the end of sentences and of some constructions that are not sentences.

9A THE PERIOD

Use a period to end a normal sentence that is not a question and is not especially emphatic.

Declarative and imperative sentences end with periods. **Declarative sentences** are those that make statements. Examples:

RIGHT: Even a dream that fails is better than no dream.
RIGHT: It is better to debate a question without settling it than to settle a question without debating it.

Imperative sentences are those that issue a request or command or give directions. Examples, with the imperative verbs italicized:

RIGHT: *Go* to the ant, thou sluggard; *consider* her ways and *be* wise.
RIGHT: *Learn* to be wise, my son, and *gladden* my heart.

There are two kinds of **indirect questions:** (1) those that simply state that someone asked something and (2) those that ask for an answer but are not phrased in question form. Periods close each kind. Examples:

RIGHT: She asked whether I could come on Tuesday.
RIGHT: I wondered whether Wednesday would be suitable.

If you quote the exact words of a question, enclose them—and the question mark—within quotation marks.

RIGHT: She asked me, "Do you have a few minutes to spare?"

If you report it as an indirect question, note that you must rephrase the original and end with a period. Use no quotation marks.

WRONG: She asked did I have a few minutes to spare.
RIGHT: She asked if I had a few minutes to spare.

Courtesy questions are those in which *will you* is equivalent to *please.* They normally are closed with periods rather than question marks, though a question mark at the end of such a sentence is not wrong. Example:

RIGHT: Will you let me know whether I need to take further action.
RIGHT: Will you let me know whether I need to take further action?

(Periods used with abbreviations are illustrated in Chapter 14.)

9B THE QUESTION MARK

Use a question mark to close a question.

Examples:

RIGHT: Where can I find the latest report?
RIGHT: Has the mail arrived already?

When a question ends a quoted part of a declarative sentence, the question mark goes inside the quotation marks and no additional period is used even though the whole is a statement rather than a question. Example:

RIGHT: The prosecuting attorney repeated, "Where were you last Tuesday night?"

When a question in a quoted part of a sentence comes first, a question mark is put inside the quotation marks but no other mark of punctuation separates the quoted part from the remainder. A period closes the whole. Example:

RIGHT: "Can I pay my telephone bill here?" the woman asked.

A question mark also is used in parentheses to indicate that the immediately preceding information is not certain or is questionable. Example:

RIGHT: The altruism (?) of some tycoons makes them richer.

Information enclosed in parentheses is followed by a question mark when the information is uncertain. Example:

RIGHT: Chaucer (born A.D. 1340?) wrote *The Canterbury Tales.*

9C THE EXCLAMATION POINT

The exclamation point (or mark) is used to close sentences or nonsentence exclamations or bits of information enclosed in parentheses when the writer wants to show strong emphasis.

Examples:

RIGHT: We will never, never yield to those insane terrorists!
RIGHT: What irony!
RIGHT: Our first week's sales of *The Reptiles* (25,000 copies!) broke all records for that kind of book.

The exclamation point, however, should be used only sparingly, for the writer who uses the mark very frequently is like the little boy crying "Wolf!" In a short time no reader will believe in the force of any of the exclamation points.

10

The Comma

Aside from marks of end punctuation, the comma is by far the most commonly used mark of punctuation and, perhaps because of that, poses more writing problems than any other mark of punctuation. Since rules for punctuation in modern English are almost wholly based on sentence structure, they are mostly precise and fixed. Some options do occur, such as using or not using, according to your pleasure, a comma to separate two short independent clauses joined by a coordinating conjunction. But we will give the basic rules and not elaborate on exceptions, for it is best for you to learn the rules and follow them before you begin to exercise options. Since there are so many rules for the use of the comma, we will use not only our number-letter system of classification but will also number the rules themselves.

In grammar, a **constituent** is any unified part of a sentence, from single words with specific grammatical functions apart from other words to various kinds of phrases and clauses.

10A CONSTITUENTS IN A SERIES

<u>Rule 1</u>   **Use commas to separate three or more constituents in a series.**

Examples (observe the comma between the last and second-to-last items):

RIGHT: On that scavenger hunt we had to collect a frog, a corset, a bottle with a rye-whisky label, a book printed in French, and a polka-dot bow tie.

RIGHT: When Roscoe will come, what he will do, and when he will leave are questions causing us profound anxiety.

If *two* constituents in a series are not joined by a coordinating conjunction, they should be separated by a comma. Example:

RIGHT: I learned to live without working, to consume without sharing.

10B COMPOUND SENTENCES

<u>Rule 2</u>   **Use a comma to separate independent clauses joined by a coordinating conjunction to form one sentence.**

The coordinating conjunctions are *and, but, yet, or, nor, for,* and *so.* Examples, with the coordinating conjunctions italicized:

RIGHT: There were too many gaps in the structure, *so* we had to tear it down and start over.

RIGHT: The Circle K Club ran the prettiest candidate for homecoming queen, *yet* she received the fewest votes.

RIGHT: The senator made astounding promises, *for* he wanted to become president.

Each clause in a compound sentence must have its own subject and predicate. Do not use a comma between the two constituents if only the subject or only the predicate is compound. Examples, with the faulty commas and conjunctions underlined:

WRONG: Neither the soup, <u>nor</u> the salad comes with the blue-plate special.

RIGHT: Neither the soup nor the salad comes with the blue-plate special.

WRONG: Carol entered the horse-judging competition, <u>and</u> took first place.

RIGHT: Carol entered the horse-judging competition and took first place.

10C INTRODUCTORY CONSTITUENTS

<u>Rule 3</u> **Use a comma to set off an introductory constituent whose meaning exhibits some separation from the sentence subject.**

Most sentences open with their subjects, but many open with a word, phrase, or clause that is not a part of the full subject. Such introductory constituents should normally be set off by commas. Examples:

RIGHT: Frankly, we all thought the assignment was too difficult.

RIGHT: Unfortunately, our plot to cancel it failed.

RIGHT: On the other hand, we did succeed in having it modified.

RIGHT: Having agreed to the change, the professor extracted a promise from us.

RIGHT: If we wanted to understand the lecture, we would at least have to complete the graph.

RIGHT: Wearing her wig and carrying an old-fashioned parasol, Madame Gagnon tottered across the lawn toward us.

Introductory adverb clauses and verbal phrases are almost always set off, as in the last two examples, since they are usually followed by a voice pause.

10D TERMINAL CONSTITUENTS

<u>Rule 4</u>   **Use a comma to set off a terminal constituent (often expressing a contrast at the end of a sentence) that is preceded by a distinct voice pause.**

Examples:

RIGHT: Ken is just eccentric, not crazy.
RIGHT: The race was run for practice, not prizes.
RIGHT: Many teen-agers are not understood by their parents, if by anyone.

(Sometimes terminal constituents are set off by dashes, as is explained in Chapter 11.)

10E PARENTHETIC CONSTITUENTS

<u>Rule 5</u>   **Use commas to set off parenthetic constituents within a sentence.**

A parenthetic constituent is a kind of aside. It is an expression that is not a part of the main sentence but that contains a comment or information that the writer wants to insert within the sentence. Some examples are *as the preacher said, according to my private sources, you will find out,* and *in the first place.* Also, conjunctive adverbs and transitional phrases that come within an independent clause are considered parenthetic. They are words and phrases such as *however, moreover, for example,* and *in fact.* Examples:

RIGHT: The highest football score ever, according to the *Guinness Book of Records*, was 222 to 0.
RIGHT: The Tories, you'll soon see, will cause a depression.
RIGHT: The way to a man's heart, Cheri discovered, is not necessarily through his stomach.
RIGHT: The moral thing to do, nevertheless, is to reveal the whole truth.
RIGHT: The evidence of demonic possession, moreover, may be mere misinterpretation of cause and effect.

10F ESSENTIAL AND NONESSENTIAL CONSTITUENTS

<u>Rule 6</u>   **Use a comma or commas to set off a nonessential constituent.**

Often a noun is followed by a modifying adjective clause or a phrase derived from such a clause, or by an appositive that renames the noun. Examples:

> Margo, *who was formerly a neighbor of mine,* loaned me
> her Jim Greeninger records. (Adjective clause)
> Ed, *finished with his education,* began looking for a job.
> (Adjective phrase)
> Helen, *my roommate,* lets me wear her clothes occasionally.
> (Appositive)

Since *Margo, Ed,* and *Helen* are proper nouns and thus are clearly identified, the expressions in italics are not necessary to establish which particular persons are meant. In that sense, the expressions are called nonessential and are set off by commas.

If, however, an adjective clause or phrase is necessary to identify which one of several is meant, the absence of commas shows that the modifier is essential. Consider this sentence:

> West Point cadets *who break the honor code* are expelled.

If the italicized adjective clause were removed, the sentence would mean that all West Point cadets are expelled. The clause is needed to identify *which* cadets are meant— only those who break the honor code. Thus no commas are called for. Now consider the following sentence:

> The Commander of West Point, *who personally investigated
> the cheating scandal,* urged leniency.

Since there is only one Commander of West Point, the term is already clearly identified. The adjective clause is nonessential and is therefore set off by commas.

The presence or absence of commas can alter meaning. Note what happens to two versions of the same sentence, one with commas and one without.

> The slide rule, which you showed me how to use, has been a help in this course.
> The slide rule which you showed me how to use has been a help in this course.

In the first sentence the commas indicate that the writer refers to the slide rule as a tool and does not mean any particular slide rule. The absence of commas in the second sentence makes the clause essential: "this particular slide rule—the one you showed me how to use."

Here are further examples, with explanations. The essential and nonessential constituents are italicized.

WRONG: Our Dean of Instruction *who was not appointed President when a vacancy occurred* decided to resign as an administrator.

RIGHT: Our Dean of Instruction, *who was not appointed President when a vacancy occurred,* decided to resign as an administrator.

The first sentence (without commas) suggests that we had more than one Dean of Instruction and that only that Dean who was not appointed President resigned. However, the word *our* already fully identifies *Dean of Instruction* (we had only one Dean), and thus the adjective clause is nonessential and must be set off by commas, as in the second sentence.

Some sentences may be correctly punctuated with or without commas, depending upon the meaning you intend to convey.

RIGHT: The students *who did most of the work building the float* were intensely pro-fraternity.

Only those students who did most of the work are meant. However, if *students* has been fully identified in a previous sentence, the adjective clause is nonessential and thus set off. Example:

RIGHT: We are surrounded by a group of students who were regaling us with odd stories about college homecomings. The students, *who did most of the work building the float,* were intensely pro-fraternity.

More examples, with adjective phrases italicized:

RIGHT (essential): The wife *happy with her lot in life* is the envy of her sisters.

RIGHT (nonessential): Mrs. Wurryfree, *happy with her lot in life,* is puzzled by the high divorce rate.

A simple test is to remove the modifying element or appositive and see if it changes the meaning of the sentence. If it does, the modifier is essential and should *not* be set off by commas. In the first sentence, only the kind of wife who is happy with her lot is meant; in the second sentence, Mrs. Wurryfree is identified by name and therefore the modifying phrase merely gives additional information.

The general rule can be summed up as follows:

essential   = no commas
nonessential = use commas

More examples, with appositives italicized:

WRONG: Raul's wife *Conchita* is president of the local Red Cross chapter.

RIGHT: Raul's wife, *Conchita,* is president of the local Red Cross chapter.

In the wrong sentence, *Conchita* is made essential, thus identifying which of Raul's wives is being mentioned. But since (presumably) Raul has only one wife, *Raul's wife* identifies her, and her name is nonessential information.

WRONG: The German writer, *Hermann Hesse,* is a favorite with college students.

RIGHT: The German writer *Hermann Hesse* is a favorite with college students.

Since Germany has more than one writer, the name is essential to identify which one is under discussion.

RIGHT: (if Morley has written only one novel): Richard Morley's novel, *Rotten in Denmark,* has sold only two hundred copies.

RIGHT: (if Morley has written more than one novel): Richard Morley's novel *Rotten in Denmark* has sold only two hundred copies.

Further typical examples of incorrectly punctuated sentences from student writing:

WRONG: Emily Dickinson wrote mostly about nature *which she felt had God-like qualities.*

WRONG: I took the case to my counselor *who backed the teacher and gave me no help at all.*

WRONG: We owe many duties to our parents *who nourish and care for us from birth until we can be self-supporting.*

WRONG: We came to the conclusion, *that it takes money to make money.*

Nature, my counselor, and *our parents* are fully identified without the italicized adjective clauses; thus the clauses, being nonessential, must be set off with commas. In the last sentence, the clause is essential to identify *conclusion* and thus the comma should *not* precede it.

Nonessential constituents may also be set off with dashes (see Chapter 11).

10G COORDINATE ADJECTIVES

<u>Rule 7</u> **Use a comma to separate coordinate adjectives which come in front of a noun and are not joined by *and*.**

The best definition of coordinate adjectives is that they are two adjectives that would sound natural if joined by *and.* If two modifiers in front of a noun will not sound natural when joined by *and,* they are not coordinate. Examples, with the adjectival modifiers italicized:

SOUNDS UNNATURAL: the *big* and *blue* station wagon
SOUNDS UNNATURAL: the *attractive* and *young* girl
SOUNDS UNNATURAL: a *wet* and *woolen* bathing suit

Since the adjectives do not sound natural with *and* joining them, they are not coordinate. With the *and* removed they would not be separated by commas. Examples:

RIGHT: the big blue station wagon
RIGHT: the attractive young girl
RIGHT: a wet woolen bathing suit

Examples of adjectives that do sound natural joined by *and:*

SOUNDS NATURAL: a *clever* and *witty* comedian
SOUNDS NATURAL: a *long* and *difficult* examination

These adjectives are coordinate and thus the normal and correct punctuation would be as follows:

RIGHT: a clever, witty comedian
RIGHT: a long, difficult examination

Of course more than two coordinate adjectives can occur in front of a noun, in which case all of them would be separated by commas, as in the following phrase:

RIGHT: a big, heavy, oblong, yellow, dirty tape dispenser

But in actuality writers do not often use more than two coordinate adjectives in front of a noun.

10H ADVERB CLAUSES

<u>Rule 8</u>   **Use a comma or commas to set off an internal or terminal adverb clause when it is separated from the rest of the sentence by a distinct voice pause or pauses.**

Introductory adverb clauses are normally set off by commas, as Rule 3 in Section 10C directs. However, since adverb clauses, which are introduced by subordinating conjunctions, cannot be clearly classified as essential or nonessential (except in the case of *when* and *where* clauses), no rule more definitive than that above can be given for punctuating them. Quite often an internal adverb clause will need to be set off because it requires distinct voice pauses. Examples:

RIGHT: The Magi, because they had seen a star in the East, made a long journey to Jerusalem.
RIGHT: Their homeward trip, once they had presented their gifts, was by another route.

A terminal adverb clause may or may not have a voice pause preceding it. In this aspect of punctuation, writers are mostly on their own with no precise rules to guide them. Example:

RIGHT: Our woodstove reduced our heating bill considerably, since we can cut our own wood in the national forest.

But change the *since* to *because* and many professional writers would feel no need for a comma. The subtleties of this aspect of punctuation are too great to be covered in a brief, elementary discussion.

10I DATES AND ADDRESSES

<u>Rule 9</u> **In full dates use a comma to separate the name of a day from the month and the date of the month from the year as well as after the number of the year.**

Examples:

RIGHT: On Sunday, April 7, 1985, many people will celebrate Easter.
RIGHT: Tuesday, June 15, 1982, marks the thirtieth wedding anniversary of our parents.

When only a month and year are given, no punctuation is necessary. Example:

RIGHT: I can find the proof I want in the June 1974 issue of *Scientific American.*

Rule 10 **In addresses use commas to separate the name of a person or establishment from the street address, the street address from the city, and the city from the state.**

Examples:

RIGHT: The parade will start in front of Hometown Hardware, 301 Adams Avenue, Joseph, Oregon, and proceed down Main Street.

RIGHT: At 1201 Elm Street, Dayton, Ohio, sits the smallest city park in the state.

10J MISUSED COMMAS

Do NOT enter an obstructive comma into any part of a sentence.

Rule 11 **Do NOT separate a subject from its verb with a single comma.**

Examples:

WRONG: The bill I support, is the one to make all beaches public property.

RIGHT: The bill I support is the one to make all beaches public property.

WRONG: That we were unwelcome, was evident.

RIGHT: That we were unwelcome was evident.

Of course a parenthetic or nonessential constituent set off on both sides may come between a subject and its verb.

Rule 12 **Do NOT separate a verb from its complement (direct object and so on) with a single comma.**

Example:

WRONG: The problem we encountered was, that we had forgotten to plug in the cord.

RIGHT: The problem we encountered was that we had forgotten to plug in the cord.

Of course a constituent set off on both sides can come between a verb and its complement. Example:

RIGHT: The problem we encountered was, believe it or not, that we had forgotten to plug in the cord.

Rule 13 Do NOT separate noncoordinate adjectives with a comma.

Examples:

WRONG: Mr. Scearce is an energetic, Baptist preacher.
RIGHT: Mr. Scearce is an energetic Baptist preacher.

WRONG: We saw the suspects in an old, blue Chevrolet.
RIGHT: We saw the suspects in an old blue Chevrolet.

Energetic and Baptist and *old and blue* would not sound natural, and thus in each instance the two modifiers are not coordinate.

Rule 14 Do NOT separate two constituents in a series joined by a coordinating conjunction.

Example:

WRONG: He insisted that we couldn't have our cake, and eat it too.
RIGHT: He insisted that we couldn't have our cake and eat it too.

11

The Dash; Parentheses; Brackets; the Colon

11A USES OF THE DASH

As a mark of punctuation, the dash has uses similar to some uses of the comma. Generally it is used when, for emphasis, the writer wants a pause slightly longer than a comma calls for or when other commas in the sentence make dashes necessary for clarity. On the typewriter a dash is made with two hyphens (--). In a sentence no space is left before or after a dash.

Rule 1   Use dashes to set off a parenthetic comment that is very long or that is a complete sentence itself.

Examples:

RIGHT: You may say many wise things—you who have lived past your allotted three score years and ten—but we young will continue to listen to our own inner voices.

RIGHT: I wrote these words—I was completely isolated at the time—when my pessimism had reached its greatest depth.

Parentheses instead of dashes would be wrong because the writers want the interpolated comments to stand out boldly rather than being an aside. Commas instead of dashes would be correct in the first example but would not provide the emphasis that the dashes do.

<u>Rule 2</u>   **Use a dash or dashes to set off a nonessential constituent that is especially emphatic or that contains commas of its own.**

Examples:

RIGHT: On my first day as a patrolman I arrested—of all people!—the mayor.
RIGHT: To our delight, Elsa's poem—brief as it was—took first prize.

In these cases the writers wanted to add emphasis to their nonessential constituents and thus used dashes instead of commas to set them off.

RIGHT: What he did in the pentathlon—the long jump, the javelin throw, the 200-meter dash, the discus throw, and the 1500-meter run—won him a gold medal.

Since the nonessential appositive has commas of its own, commas to set it off would cause confusion. Dashes provide clarity.

<u>Rule 3</u>   **Use a dash to give emphasis to a constituent that would not normally be set off at all.**

Example:

RIGHT: Those corrupt politicians deserve credit for giving Americans an overdue—and much-needed—civics lesson.

And much-needed need not be set off at all, but the writer set it off with dashes in order to emphasize it. Commas would provide some emphasis but not as much as dashes.

<u>Rule 4</u>   **Use a dash to set off a terminal constituent that is an explanation of a preceding constituent or that is a very distinct afterthought.**

Examples:

RIGHT: Strawn resorted to his only hope—plea bargaining.
RIGHT: The best way to settle an argument is to speak softly—
or buy drinks all around.

In the first example, a colon after *hope* would also be correct but more formal. In the second example, only a dash will produce the delayed-afterthought effect the writer wanted.

<u>Rule 5</u>   **Use a dash to set off an initial series of constituents which is then summarized by a noun or pronoun that serves as the sentence subject.**

Example:

RIGHT: The dinosaur, the saber-toothed tiger, the dodo bird—
all have become extinct.

The pronoun *all* is used to summarize the initial constituents in order to emphasize them.

    Caution: Do *not* use dashes instead of periods as end punctuation.

11B USES OF PARENTHESES

The word *parentheses* is plural, meaning both the curved marks that go by that name (*parenthesis* is the singular). A space is used outside a parenthesis unless another mark of punctuation follows it, but no space is used on the inside of a parenthesis. If an entire sentence following a mark of end punctuation is enclosed in parentheses, the period to close the sentence goes inside the final parenthesis. If only the terminal part of a sentence is enclosed in parentheses, the period closing the sentence goes outside the parenthesis. If a complete sentence enclosed in parentheses does not come after a mark of end punctuation, the period closing the entire sentence goes outside the parenthesis.

<u>Rule 6</u> **Use parentheses to enclose any kind of parenthetic or nonessential constituent—even a sentence or group of sentences—when such a constituent has a tone of isolation from the main sentence and is intended to be an aside.**

Example:

RIGHT: We continued to frolic with carefree abandon (later we would learn that we had troubles).

The writer does not intend to discuss the troubles at this point; hence the parenthetic comment is in parentheses, which isolate it more than a dash would. Note that the period closing the whole sentence goes outside the parenthesis because the nonenclosed sentence does not have end punctuation. Another correct way of punctuating this construction is this:

RIGHT: We continued to frolic with careless abandon. (Later we would learn that we had troubles.)

RIGHT: In 1933 Norris Baxter (later to become a movie star) attracted much attention with his theory of orgones.

Parentheses rather than dashes or commas set off this constituent because it has a tone of isolation or is somewhat of an afterthought or an aside.

RIGHT: Both Turner and Avinger were refusing to sign contracts. (Grady and Towle had signed as early as February, but they were hardly star players. Tooey had signed, too, but he alone could not constitute a pitching staff.) Not only were they asking for huge salary increases but also for other concessions. . . .

The enclosed two sentences are an aside, not directly a part of the discussion of Turner and Avinger. Note that the *they* of the last sentence refers to Turner and Avinger, not to the names within the parentheses. Also note that the period goes inside the parentheses because complete sentences are enclosed.

<u>Rule 7</u>   **Use parentheses to enclose numerals used to number items in a series.**

Example:

RIGHT: Writing a compelling essay includes **(1)** choosing and limiting a subject, **(2)** determining the thesis, **(3)** organizing the material, **(4)** writing the first draft, **(5)** editing and revising, and **(6)** proofreading after preparing the final manuscript.

Note that the conjunction *and* precedes the parentheses that enclose the last item.

<u>Rule 8</u>   **Use parentheses to enclose cross-references and bits of information inserted so as not to be a part of the grammatical structure of the sentence.**

Example:

RIGHT: Calvinism **(**see also Puritanism**)** has as its charter the famous *Institutes of the Christian Religion* by John Calvin **(**1509 – 1564**)**.

The first enclosure is a cross-reference. The second enclosure is information—birth and death dates—that the writer wanted to insert without composing another sentence or large constituent in order to do so.

11C   USES OF BRACKETS

Square brackets [like the ones enclosing this phrase] should not be confused with parentheses.

<u>Rule 9</u>   **Use brackets to enclose nonquoted material inserted into a direct quotation for the purpose of clarification.**

Example:

RIGHT: The article continues: "Five years after filing the suit **[**_Bono_ vs. _Saxbe_**]** life has changed little."

The writer uses a direct quotation, but the readers would not have known the reference of *suit*. Therefore the reference is given in brackets for clarification.

Rule 10 **Use brackets to enclose comments inserted into direct quotations.**

Such insertions may be information included to make a quotation intelligible or personal comments. Examples:

RIGHT: His answer read as follows: "Sourcasim [sic] is a form of irony."

The word *sic* means *thus* and is used by the writer to indicate that the error was in the original quotation.

RIGHT: "Bailey insists [as he naturally would] that the committee will stay clear of politics."

Here the writer wanted to insert a personal comment at the appropriate place rather than to delay the comment until the quotation was ended.

11D USES OF THE COLON

The colon is a mark of punctuation used to introduce various kinds of constituents or longer passages of discourse.

Rule 11 **Use a colon after the salutation in a formal letter.**

Examples:

FORMAL: Dear Professor Burnsides:
INFORMAL: Dear Millie,

Rule 12 **Use a colon after an introductory label.**

Examples:

INCORRECT: Peel them potatoes.
CORRECT: Peel those potatoes.

<u>Rule 13</u>   **Use a colon to introduce a series that is prepared for in the main clause of a sentence.**

Example:

RIGHT: My deductions were as follows: the student has a photographic memory; she had read the chapter carefully; in her term paper she unconsciously used the wording of the original as though it were her own.

<u>Rule 14</u>   **A colon may be used after a sentence that introduces a direct quotation.**

Example:

RIGHT: It was William James who said: "To *know* is one thing, and to know for certain *that* we know is another. One may hold to the first being possible without the second."

<u>Rule 15</u>   **A colon may be used to introduce a terminal constituent that is an explanation.**

Example:

RIGHT: One thing remained to be done: submitting the report.

A dash after *done* would also be correct, though more informal.

<u>Rule 16</u>   **Do NOT use a colon directly after the verbs *are* and *were*.**

Instead, use no punctuation at all, or use such a word as *these* or *the following* after *are* or *were* and before the colon. Examples:

POOR STYLE: The facts in the case were: the defendant had not been advised of his rights; the arresting officer had used unnecessary force; and the crime violated a law that had not been invoked for over fifty years.

PROPER STYLE: The facts in the case were the following: the defendant had not been advised of his rights; the arresting officer had used unnecessary force; and the crime violated a law that had not been invoked for over fifty years.

WRONG: The most distant planets are: Uranus, Neptune, and Pluto.

RIGHT: The most distant planets are Uranus, Neptune, and Pluto.

WRONG: The reasons we gave for coming late were: our alarm clock failed to ring, our car failed to start at first, and our driver foolishly tried a shortcut he didn't know well.

RIGHT: The reasons we gave for coming late were these: our alarm clock failed to ring, our car failed to start at first, and our driver foolishly tried a shortcut he didn't know well.

12

The Semicolon

A general rule is that semicolons are used to separate only coordinate, not noncoordinate, constituents. The semicolon calls for a voice pause as long as that of a period, but it is used only as internal punctuation.

12A COMPOUND SENTENCES WITHOUT CONNECTIVES

Rule 1   Use a semicolon to separate two independent clauses that form a compound sentence but that do not have a connective word between them.

Examples:

RIGHT: Our house is progressing nicely; the carpenters have already hung the doors.

RIGHT: Sixteen men had applied; we could choose only one for the position.

Writers use such compound sentences because they do not want to separate such closely related clauses into separate sentences. Note particularly that semicolons are required between the clauses; commas would produce comma splices (see Chapter 3).

12B COMPOUND SENTENCES WITH CONNECTIVES

<u>Rule 2</u> **Use a semicolon to separate two independent clauses joined by a connective other than a coordinating conjunction.**

When independent clauses are joined by a coordinating conjunction, they usually need only a comma between them. When they are connected by a conjunctive adverb or a transitional phrase, they must be separated by a semicolon unless they are punctuated as separate sentences. Sometimes the conjunctive adverb or transitional phrase is shifted to the interior of the second clause. Examples:

RIGHT: Lisa recently announced her engagement; however, she hasn't set the date for the wedding yet.
RIGHT: The nation was mourning the death of the emperor; the flags, consequently, were all at half-mast.

The semicolons in these examples are necessary, unless each example were punctuated as two sentences. Commas in place of the semicolons would produce comma splices (see Chapter 3).

12C CONSTITUENTS IN A SERIES

<u>Rule 3</u> **Use semicolons to separate constituents in a series when the constituents have internal punctuation of their own or when the constituents are especially long.**

Examples:

RIGHT: The participants divided themselves into three groups: (1) philosophers, theologians, and linguists; (2) poets, novelists, and dramatists; and (3) historians, economists, and geographers.

Since each of the three parts of the series has commas of its own, semicolons clarify the structure. Note that the semicolons still separate coordinate constituents. Also note that this example illustrates one use of the colon and one use of parentheses.

RIGHT: Professor Means's study showed that American Indians from reservations made lower average scores on standardized tests than Indians living off reservations; that Indians who live in a stable community scored higher than those who are migrant; and that Indians tested in their own languages scored higher on I.Q. tests than Indians tested in English.

Because the constituents in a series in this example are so long, the semicolons make the sentence structure clearer than commas would, though commas would be acceptable.

12D MISUSED SEMICOLONS

<u>Rule 4</u> **Do NOT use a semicolon between non-coordinate constituents.**

Example:

WRONG: The speech tournament had been exhausting; especially the demanding debate at the end.
RIGHT: The speech tournament had been exhausting, especially the demanding debate at the end.

A comma should replace the semicolon since the second constituent is not an independent clause and thus is not coordinate with the constituent that precedes the semicolon.

Rule 5 Do NOT use a semicolon after the connective *such as.*

Example:

WRONG: I dislike several foods that are supposed to be good for me, such as; broccoli, spinach, and green peppers.

RIGHT: I dislike several foods that are supposed to be good for me, such as broccoli, spinach, and green peppers.

Rule 6 Do NOT use a semicolon in place of a dash or colon.

Examples:

WRONG: Just one thing kept me from carrying out my plan; lack of money.

RIGHT: Just one thing kept me from carrying out my plan— lack of money.

WRONG: Neapolitan sherbet usually comes in three flavors; vanilla, orange, and strawberry.

RIGHT: Neapolitan sherbet usually comes in three flavors: vanilla, orange, and strawberry.

13

Quotation Marks

13A DIRECT QUOTATIONS

<u>Rule 1</u> **Enclose direct quotations in quotation marks.**

Examples:

RIGHT: Howard remarked, "We can easily make it through that mudhole."

RIGHT: "I don't think I would try it if I were you," cautioned Angie.

These are straightforward examples of the exact words each speaker used. *Howard remarked* and *cautioned Angie* are the introductory expressions, even though one appears at the beginning and the other at the end of the sentences. Note the capitalization and the use of commas.

RIGHT: Feuer maintained that **"**a minority of students are turning to shallow faculties on the outskirts of the universities where a variety of [charlatans] . . . offer courses in which they provide answers as well as questions.**"**

This is the kind of direct quotation that might appear in a term paper. Since the quotation forms an integral part of the sentence structure, no comma follows *Feuer maintained that.* (Note that square brackets enclose material not in the direct quotation but interjected by the writer for clarification. Also note that three spaced periods indicate ellipsis, or omission of part of the quotation.)

RIGHT: He maintained that children are **"**credulous**"** and **"**unresistant to indoctrination.**"**

When such a connective as *and* joins two quoted units, as in the above example, each quoted unit is enclosed in quotation marks but the unquoted connective word is not.

RIGHT: Rodney asked, **"**Will you join the organization?**"**
"No.**"**
"Then you must not repeat anything you have heard tonight.**"**

This is an example of direct quotations as they are used in dialogue in fiction. The words of each new speaker appear in a separate paragraph.

13B QUOTATIONS WITHIN QUOTATIONS

<u>Rule 2</u> **When a direct quotation is used within a direct quotation, enclose the internal quotation in single quotation marks and the whole quotation in regular quotation marks.**

Example:

RIGHT: The commencement speaker said: **"**In Ecclesiastes we read that **'**In much wisdom is much grief, and he who increaseth knowledge increaseth sorrow,**'** but we must still pursue knowledge for the fulfillment of God's will.**"**

Also the constituents covered in Rules 3, 4, 5, and 6 in Sections 13C and 13D should be enclosed in single quotation marks if they appear within a direct quotation.

13C TITLES

Rule 3 **Use quotation marks to enclose the quoted titles of short stories, short poems, one-act plays, essays, chapters, and other literary works of less than book or three-act-play length.**

Examples:

RIGHT: E. A. Robinson's poem "Mr. Flood's Party" is about an old man who has outlived his time.

RIGHT: "The Capital of the World" is one of Hemingway's best stories.

RIGHT: The third chapter of *The Scarlet Letter* is entitled "The Recognition."

RIGHT: Professor Lucy Phurr distinctly said, "Read Melville's short story 'Bartleby the Scrivener' by tomorrow."

Note the single quotation marks enclosing the title in the last example.

Titles of book-length literary works (*The Scarlet Letter* in the third example) are underlined in longhand and italicized in print (see Section 14B). No title should ever be both underlined and enclosed in quotation marks.

Rule 4 **Do NOT put quotation marks around a title used as the heading of a theme or essay.**

Of course if a quoted unit is included in the title, that unit is enclosed in quotation marks. Examples:

TITLE AS HEADING: How Nellie Paid the Mortgage on the Farm

TITLE AS HEADING: A Study of Christian Symbols in Steinbeck's "The Flight"

If the second title appeared in a paragraph, the whole title would be in regular quotation marks and the title of the story in single quotation marks.

13D   SPECIAL CONSTITUENTS

<u>Rule 5</u>   **A word used as a word and not for its meaning may be enclosed in quotation marks.**

Examples:

RIGHT: Both "tomato" and "tart" are commonly used as slang terms.
RIGHT: Ling Chan's proposal contained too many "if's."

Such words used as words may instead be underlined in longhand and italicized in print (see Section 14B), but never are they both underlined and put in quotation marks.

<u>Rule 6</u>   **Use quotation marks to enclose a word or phrase used in a special or ironical sense.**

Examples:

RIGHT: Mona feels that she must belong to the "right set."
RIGHT: The "justice" of the verdict was enough to make me cry.

In the first example, the quotation marks show that the writer does not believe as Mona does—that only the set she belongs to is special or worthy of praise. In the second example, the quotation marks mean that the writer does not think the verdict represents justice at all.

You should avoid enclosing slang terms in quotation marks as an apology for their use. If a slang term is worth using, use it without apology. Example:

POOR USAGE: Claudette has a "hang-up" about rich boys trying to date her.
BETTER: Claudette has a hang-up about rich boys trying to date her.

13E   WITH OTHER MARKS OF PUNCTUATION

<u>Rule 7</u> **Always put periods and commas inside rather than outside quotation marks, regardless of whether the period or comma belongs to the quoted unit.**

Examples:

RIGHT: I entitled my paper "Existentialism in *Moby Dick*."

RIGHT: Although our preacher says "The way of the transgressor is hard," I notice that our local crooks have an easy time of it.

Neither the period in the first example nor the comma in the second belongs to the quoted unit, but each is correctly placed within the quotation marks.

<u>Rule 8</u> **Marks of punctuation other than the period and the comma are placed inside quotation marks when they are a part of the quoted unit and outside the quotation marks when they are not a part of the quoted unit.**

Examples:

RIGHT: Did Professor Gallegos say "to chapter ten" or "through chapter ten"?

Since the question mark does not belong to the quoted unit, it is placed outside the quotation marks.

RIGHT: Ann Landers was heard to utter, "Why am I so lonely?"

Since the question mark belongs to the quoted unit, it is placed inside the quotation marks. Note also that no additional period is used even though the whole sentence is a statement and not a question.

RIGHT: Franklin said, "He who hesitates is lost"; he also said, "Look before you leap."

The semicolon is not a part of the quoted unit and thus is placed outside the quotation marks.

14

Mechanics

14A MANUSCRIPT FORM

14A1 For Handwritten Papers

Observe the following directions in preparing handwritten papers:

1. Use blue or black ink, if possible. Never use colored inks or perfumed inks.
2. Write on lined 8½ × 11 notebook paper. Cut off edges of paper torn from a spiral notebook.
3. To allow for corrections and comments, many instructors require that you skip every other line—especially for out-of-class assignments. Avoid narrow-spaced paper, if possible.
4. Write on one side of the paper only.
5. Compose a title (not just a statement of the topic) for your paper. Skip a line between the title and the first line of your paper.

6. Do *not* enclose your title in quotation marks, *do not* underline it, and *do not* use a period. (Titles do not ordinarily have end punctuation.) A unit within the title, such as the title of a short story or a word used in a special sense (see Section 13D), should be enclosed in quotation marks. The title of a book within your paper's title should be underlined.

7. Do not write outside the left-hand margin line (usually in red, if there is one), except to put numbers of questions if you are writing a test.

8. Leave at least a one-inch margin on the right-hand side of your notebook paper and at the bottom; do not crowd the right-hand side nor write down the right-hand margin. However, do not leave an excessively wide right-hand margin.

9. Use a hyphen to divide a word at the end of a line and divide *only* between syllables. Do *not* divide a one-syllable word, such as *twel-ve* or *walk-ed*. Do *not* divide a word so that a single letter is set apart, such as *a-bove* or *pun-y*. Consult a dictionary, if necessary, for syllabification.

10. Never let a mark of end punctuation, a comma, a semicolon, or a colon begin a line of your paper. Never end a line with the first of a set of quotation marks, parentheses, or brackets.

11. Indent each paragraph about one inch.

12. It is acceptable to draw a single line through an error and to write the correction neatly above it. Recopy a page that contains more than two errors. Try to make every physical aspect of your paper neat. Proofread carefully.

13. Follow your instructor's directions for folding your paper and entering your name and other information on it.

14A2   For Typewritten Papers

Observe the following directions in preparing typewritten papers:

1. Use unruled 8½ × 11 bond paper, if possible. Do not use onionskin paper.
2. Avoid using a red-ink ribbon. Type on one side of the paper only.
3. For your title, follow directions 5 and 6 in Section 14A1.
4. Double-space between the lines of your paper (except for inset quotations and footnotes in a term paper).
5. Double-space horizontally (that is, use two typewriter spaces instead of one) after all marks of end punctuation and colons.
6. Single-space after commas, semicolons, parentheses, and brackets.
7. Make a dash with two hyphens (--) and leave no space before or after a dash.
8. When underlining to show italics, underline the spaces between words too, unless your instructor gives you different instructions.
9. To make the numeral 1, use the small letter l on the keyboard, *not* the capital i.
10. Do not number page one; place page numbers in the upper right-hand corners of succeeding pages. Use Arabic numerals (2, 3, 4, and so on) rather than Roman numerals (II, III, IV, and so on) to number pages.
11. Follow direction 9 in Section 14A1 for dividing words at the end of a line.
12. Maintain a 1¼-inch margin on the left-hand side of each page and about a one-inch margin on the other three sides. Of course the right-hand ends of lines in typewriting, as in longhand, will be uneven.
13. Indent paragraphs five spaces.
14. Keep your paper neat and proofread it carefully.
15. Follow your instructor's directions for folding your paper and entering your name and other information on it.

14B   UNDERLINING AND QUOTATION MARKS

Underlining in longhand or typing is equivalent to italics in print. Underlining and quotation marks are linked in certain ways.

14B1   Underlining

<u>Rule 1</u>   **Underline titles of book-length literary works, newspapers, magazines, works of art, musical compositions, and names of ships and aircraft.**

Examples:

RIGHT: Mark Twain's Tom Sawyer
         Shakespeare's <u>Romeo and Juliet</u>
         Milton's <u>Paradise Lost</u>
         <u>Harper's</u> magazine (Only the name of the magazine is underlined.)
         the Los Angeles <u>Times</u> (The city is not usually underlined.)
         Handel's <u>The Messiah</u> (a musical composition)
         Degas's <u>The Dancer and the Bouquet</u> (a painting)
         the <u>Titanic</u> (a ship)
         <u>Air Force One</u> (an individual aircraft)

<u>Rule 2</u>   **Underline foreign words and phrases that have not been fully Anglicized.**

Consult a dictionary if necessary. Examples:

RIGHT: The <u>sine qua non</u> of science is accuracy.
RIGHT: The <u>raison d'être</u> of freshman composition is employment for English teachers.

<u>Rule 3</u>   **Words or phrases used as words or phrases and not for their meaning may be underlined.**

Examples:

RIGHT: The slang phrase <u>out of sight</u> originated in the nineteenth century.

RIGHT: Professor Stone's inaccurate use of <u>epistemology</u> confused his students.

Words used as words may be enclosed in quotation marks, but they are never both underlined and enclosed in quotation marks.

<u>Rule 4</u> **Words or phrases may be underlined for emphasis.**

Examples:

RIGHT: I kept quiet precisely because I <u>didn't</u> want the defendant found not guilty.

RIGHT: For human survival we <u>must</u> discontinue all arms manufacturing.

Single words or short phrases, such as *not,* may be capitalized, instead of underlined, for emphasis. However, underlining or capitalization for emphasis should be used judiciously, for overuse will cause readers to lose faith in the need for emphasis.

14B2 Quotation Marks

The use of quotation marks for enclosing direct quotations is covered in Chapter 13. Here we discuss these marks only as they are related to underlining (italics). Periods and commas are always put inside quotation marks, even when they are not a part of the quoted unit. Other marks of punctuation are put inside quotation marks when they are part of the quoted unit and outside when they are not part of the quoted unit. See Section 13E for examples.

<u>Rule 5</u> **Use quotation marks to enclose titles of short stories, short poems, one-act plays, essays, chapters, and other literary works of less than book or three-act-play length.**

RIGHT: Frost's poem "Birches"
Faulkner's short story "That Evening Sun"
Fred Jacobs's short play "Golden Land"
Thoreau's essay "Civil Disobedience"
Chapter 14 is entitled "The Campaign of '48."

Underlining identifies major works or separate publications. Quotation marks are reserved for lesser works or parts of major works. No title is ever both underlined and enclosed in quotation marks.

Do not put a title used as a heading in quotation marks.

Units within the title as heading may, however, be enclosed in quotation marks. Examples:

TITLE AS HEADING: Abroad with Two Yanks
TITLE AS HEADING: The History of "Gab" as Slang

<u>Rule 7</u>   **A word or phrase used as a word or phrase and not for its meaning may be enclosed in quotation marks.**

Examples:

RIGHT: "Biddable" is one of the most euphonious words in English.
RIGHT: The expression "rattle your cage" is a merging of two slang terms.

Also, words used as words may be underlined, but never both underlined and enclosed in quotation marks.

<u>Rule 8</u>   **Use quotation marks to enclose a word or phrase used in a special ironic sense.**

Example:

RIGHT: Bernie likes to think he is a member of the "literary" set.

The quotation marks mean that the writer does not think Bernie's set has real literary attributes.

14C   ABBREVIATIONS

Rules for using abbreviations vary considerably, as you will observe in your reading. The rules given here are an acceptable guide for the sort of writing done in English composition courses. They do not apply to such writing as addresses on envelopes, lists, technical data, and other special forms of composition.

14C1 Abbreviations Acceptable in All Kinds of Writing

<u>Rule 9</u> **Use the following abbreviations designating individuals:**

Mr.
Mrs.
Ms. (any female)
Messrs. (plural of Mr.)
Mmes. (plural of Mrs.)
St. (Saint)
Sr.
Jr.

<u>Rule 10</u> **Use abbreviations to designate any earned or honorary degrees or special awards.**

Examples:

DEGREES: A.B.
B.A.
M.A.
M.D. (medical doctor)
Ph.D. (doctor of philosophy)
Ed.D. (doctor of education)
D.D.S. (doctor of dental science)
D.D. (doctor of divinity)
J.D. (doctor of jurisprudence)
D.V.M. (doctor of veterinary medicine)
D.Lit. *or* D.Litt. (doctor of literature)
LL.D. (doctor of laws)
D.H.L. (doctor of Hebrew literature)

SPECIAL AWARDS: O.M. (Order of Merit: English)
D.S.C. (Distinguished Service Cross)
D.S.M. (Distinguished Service Medal)

<u>Rule 11</u>   **Use the following abbreviations designating time:**

1800 B.C. (before Christ)
A.D. 1462 (in the year of our Lord)
DST, PST (daylight saving time, Pacific standard time, and so on)
4:12 A.M. *or* 4:12 a.m.
3:30 P.M. *or* 3:30 p.m.

<u>Rule 12</u>   **Use abbreviations to designate well-known agencies, organizations, and unions, either governmental or private.**

Examples:

UN	CIA
UNESCO	VA
WHO	VFW
CARE	ILGWU
CAB	UAW

While such abbreviations usually appear with no periods, you may use periods if you wish. The important thing is to be consistent and to make sure your usage will be clear to the reader.

<u>Rule 13</u>   **Frequently used technical terms may be abbreviated.**

Examples:

mpg (miles per gallon)   rpm (revolutions per minute)
mph (miles per hour)   Btu (British thermal unit)

<u>Rule 14</u>   **The abbreviations *no., nos.,* and $ are acceptable when used with numerals.**

Examples:

RIGHT: The winner was no. 4238.
RIGHT: Please pay particular attention to nos. 2, 6, 9, and 13.
RIGHT: My plumbing bill was $1239.62.

<u>Rule 15</u>   **The following abbreviations of standard foreign phrases may be used.**

i.e. (that is)   *viz.* (namely)
e.g. (for example)   *cf.* (compare with)
c. or *ca.* (*circa:* about)

Rule 16   **In purely technical writing abbreviations of technical terms are acceptable.**

Examples:

cc. (cubic centimeter)   gm. (gram)
cm. (centimeter)   in. (inch)

The examples in the above eight rules are representative. Other abbreviations of the same sort are acceptable. When in doubt, consult a dictionary.

14C2   Abbreviations to Be Avoided in Semiformal Writing

Rule 17   **Avoid abbreviating titles of individuals** (except as specified in Section 14C1, Rule 9).

Examples:

WRONG: The *Pres.* will hold a press conference today.
RIGHT: The **President** will hold a press conference today.

WRONG: The committee includes *Prof.* Dingbat and *Sen.* Jonas.
RIGHT: The committee includes **Professor** Dingbat and **Senator** Jonas.

Rule 18   **Avoid abbreviating first names.**

Examples:

WRONG: Benj.   Geo.   Jas.   Theo.

Rule 19   **Avoid abbreviating the names of states, provinces, and countries.**

Examples:

WRONG: The Holdens went to *N.Y.* for their vacation.
RIGHT: The Holdens went to **New York** for their vacation.

WRONG: Professor Ainsley spent her sabbatical in *Eng.*
RIGHT: Professor Ainsley spent her sabbatical in **England.**

Rule 20   Avoid abbreviating the names of days, months, and seasons.

Examples:

WRONG: The last day of *Feb.* falls on a *Thurs.* this year.
RIGHT: The last day of **February** falls on a **Thursday** this year.

Rule 21   Avoid abbreviating names of streets, avenues, boulevards, and courts.

Examples:

WRONG: Phil just bought a house on Baylor *St.*
RIGHT: Phil just bought a house on Baylor **Street.**

Rule 22   Avoid abbreviating the word *company* and avoid the ampersand (&), unless it is part of the name of a firm.

Examples:

WRONG: the Johnsons & the Smollets
RIGHT: the Johnsons **and** the Smollets

WRONG: T. L. Floyd *& Co.* is an equal-opportunity employer.
RIGHT: T. L. Floyd **& Company** is an equal-opportunity employer.

Rule 23   Avoid the abbreviation Xmas.

Rule 24   Avoid abbreviating weights and measurements.

Examples:

WRONG:	RIGHT:
oz.	ounce *or* ounces
lbs.	pounds
ft.	foot *or* feet
yds.	yards

Rule 25   Avoid abbreviating common words.

Examples:

WRONG: yrs.   RIGHT: years *or* yours
      bldg.   building
      sch.   school
      Rom. C.   Roman Catholic
      con't.   continued
      gov't.   government

14D NUMERALS

Although usage varies, the following rules for the use of numerals and spelled-out numbers are a satisfactory guide.

<u>Rule 26</u> **For random figures, spell out numbers that require no more than two words; use numerals for numbers that would require more than two words if spelled out.**

Examples:

PREFERRED: Over **three thousand** years ago Daedalus tried to fly, but man has succeeded in only the last **seventy-five.**

PREFERRED: The companies expected sales of **seven million;** their exact total amounted to **6,398,207.**

PREFERRED: Each year there are **174** days between Independence Day and Christmas.

In the second example, note the use of commas without spaces in the large figure written in numerals.

<u>Rule 27</u> **In a sentence or passage that contains a series of figures, use numerals for all of them.**

Example:

PREFERRED: My unit sales for each of my first seven workdays were **9, 22, 8, 101, 61, 3,** and **102.**

Note that the word *seven* is written out, since it is not part of the series.

<u>Rule 28</u>   **Use numerals in dates, addresses, and time when accompanied by A.M. or P.M.**

Examples:

RIGHT: July **11, 1922** *or* **11** July **1922** (military and technical style)
RIGHT: **242** Columbus Street, Apartment **3B**
RIGHT: Room **701,** Hotel Padre
RIGHT: **8:22** A.M.

On checks and other such writing, dates may be written in this way: 7-11-22 *or* 7/11/22.

<u>Rule 29</u>   **Use numerals to state measurements, page numbers, and money used with $.**

Examples:

RIGHT: You'll find **4″ x 6″** cards more convenient than **3″ x 5″** cards for library notes.
RIGHT: The point of the gable was **13′6″** from the floor.
RIGHT: You'll find answers on pages **386** through **407.**
RIGHT: The net cost per unit was **$18.73.**

But when simple, nonfractional numbers are involved, they may be spelled out. Examples:

RIGHT: Our rival's center is nearly **seven** feet tall.
RIGHT: We expect **twenty dollars** to be sufficient.

<u>Rule 30</u>   **When decimals or fractions are involved, use numerals.**

Examples:

RIGHT: Last year the rainfall was **4.11** inches above normal.
RIGHT: The prime rate exceeded **20¼** percent in 1980.

<u>Rule 31</u>   **Use numerals for code numbers, such as Social Security numbers, air flight numbers, and telephone numbers.**

Examples:

RIGHT: We needed kit number **4307884** to rebuild the carburetor.
RIGHT: Call **963-2171,** extension **250,** to register.

Rule 32   **To prevent misreading when two numbers appear consecutively, spell out the first one and use numerals for the other.**

Example:

RIGHT: I caught **six 8-inch** trout.

Rule 33   **Except in purely technical writing, do not open a sentence with numerals.**

Examples:

POOR STYLE: *1250* partisan voters attended the rally.
PREFERRED: **Twelve hundred and fifty** partisan voters attended the rally.

Rule 34   **Except in legal and commercial writing, it is not good style to enter numerals in parentheses after a spelled-out number.**

Example:

INAPPROPRIATE STYLE: I purchased *twenty-five (25)* paperback books at the College Bookstore's recent sale.
BETTER: I purchased **twenty-five** paperback books. . . .

14E   CONTRACTIONS

Nowadays, contractions such as *won't, doesn't, shouldn't,* and so on appear in semiformal writing in such magazines as *Harper's, Consumer Reports,* and *Science News* and in many books of nonfiction. Opinion among English teachers, however, is divided as to whether contractions should be allowed in writing assigned in college composition courses. You should ascertain your instructor's preference and follow it.

SECTION THREE

SPELLING

15

Spelling Rules

English spelling is, as everyone knows, full of irregularities which make spelling a difficult subject. But there is much regularity in our spelling system, too, and the irregularities are for the most part rather narrowly limited. For example, the sound /f/ is not always spelled *f,* but it is always spelled either *f* (as in *fit*), *ff* (as in *buff*), *ph* (as in *photo*), or *gh* (as in *laugh*) and so has a degree of regularity. Thus, though English spelling is hard and most people have trouble with it, an understanding of its regularities can improve anyone's spelling. There are several spelling rules that are highly useful to everyone who masters them, for they give much insight into the regularities of English spelling. (There are spelling rules other than those that follow, but they are so riddled with exceptions and so hard to remember that they are not very useful.)

15A THE DOUBLING-OF-THE-FINAL-CONSONANT RULE

The doubling-of-the-final-consonant rule is complex but applies to a great many common words. The rule:

<u>Rule 1</u>   **When adding a suffix beginning with a vowel to a word which is accented on the last syllable and which ends in a single consonant preceded by a single vowel, double the final consonant.**

The accented or stressed syllable is the one spoken with most force. For example, we accent the last syllable of *re-FER,* but we accent the first syllable of *SUF-fer.*

This complicated rule is based on an important phonetic principle in English spelling called the long-vowel, short-vowel principle, which has two parts. First, in a vowel-consonant-vowel sequence the first vowel, *if it is in an accented syllable,* is long. Thus in *debate* the a-t-e sequence in the accented syllable causes the *a* to be long. Second, in a vowel–final consonant sequence or a vowel-consonant-consonant sequence, the vowel is short. Thus in *bat* the a-t sequence at the end makes the *a* short; also in *batted* the a-t-t sequence keeps the *a* short. There are, inevitably in English, many exceptions to this principle, but it is regular enough to be highly useful, both in understanding the doubling-of-the-final-consonant rule (which is almost always regular) and in understanding many other words. For example, a great many people misspell *occasion* by using two *s*'s instead of one, which misspelling would give the pronunciation *o-KASS-yun* instead of the correct *o-KAY-zyun.* Understanding the long-vowel, short-vowel principle prevents such mistakes. Here are more examples of the principle at work:

long vowels	*short vowels*
rate	rat
Pete	pet
bite	bit
rote	rot
cure	cur

In the first column the silent *e*'s—forming a vowel-consonant-vowel sequence—make the first vowel long. In the second column the vowels are short because the second consonant ends the word. The whole purpose of the doubling-of-the-final-consonant rule is to preserve the short vowel sound in such words as *dis-BAR, re-FER, ad-MIT,* and *dot* when a suffix beginning with a vowel is added to them. (The letters *a* and *e* have more than one short-vowel sound so far as this rule is concerned.)

Since the rule is complex, here again are the three main parts of it:

1. The suffix added must begin with a vowel. Such suffixes are *ing, ed, er, est, able, y,* and so on.
2. The word to which the suffix is added must be accented on the last syllable. All one-syllable words and such words as *pre-FER, oc-CUR,* and *com-PEL* are examples.
3. The word to which the suffix is added must end in a single consonant preceded by a single vowel. *Admit, repel,* and *slap* are examples. *Equip* and *quit* are examples too, since the *qu* really stands for the consonant sound *kw,* leaving the single vowel *i* before the final consonant.

When the above three conditions are present, the final consonant is doubled and the short vowel sound is retained.

Here are some doubling-of-the-final-consonant words that are frequently misspelled:

admit + ed = admi**tt**ed
begin + er = begi**nn**er
begin + ing = begi**nn**ing
brag + ing = bra**gg**ing
confer + ed = confe**rr**ed
defer + ed = defe**rr**ed
equip + ed = equi**pp**ed
expel + ed = expe**ll**ed
fad + ism = fa**dd**ism
fog + y = fo**gg**y

jog + ing = jo**gg**ing
lag + ing = la**gg**ing
man + ish = ma**nn**ish
occur + ed = occu**rr**ed
occur + ence = occu**rr**ence
omit + ed = omi**tt**ed
rebel + ing = rebe**ll**ing
red + est = re**dd**est
refer + ed = refe**rr**ed
regret + ed = regre**tt**ed
star + ing = sta**rr**ing
swim + ing = swi**mm**ing
transfer + ed = transfe**rr**ed
(un)forget + able = unforge**tt**able

Two notes of caution: (1) If the last syllable of a word is not accented, its final consonant is not doubled when a suffix beginning with a vowel is added. Examples:

aBANdon + ed = abandoned   BANter + ing = bantering
proHIBit + ing = prohibiting   BENefit + ed = benefited

(2) When a suffix is added to a word ending in a silent *e,* the consonant preceding the *e* is *never* doubled. Examples:

come + ing = coming   shine + ing = shining
dine + ing = dining   write + ing = writing
interfere + ed = interfered

These five words are very frequently misspelled because the consonants preceding the silent *e*'s are incorrectly doubled.

15B THE DROPPING-OF-THE-SILENT-E RULE

A great many words in English end in a silent *e.* When suffixes are added to these words, sometimes the *e* is dropped and sometimes it is retained. In this section we will consider the rule calling for the dropping of the silent *e,* and in the next, the rules calling for retention of the *e.* The basic silent *e* rule is this:

<u>Rule 2</u>   **When adding a suffix beginning with a vowel to a word ending in a silent e, drop the silent e.**

One of the rules in the following section is an important exception to this basic rule, but we must explain the rules separately.

    The dropping-of-the-silent *e* rule is also due to the long-vowel, short-vowel principle discussed in the preceding section. Though there are exceptions, most terminal silent *e*'s are doing the job of making the preceding vowel long. That is, if the silent *e* is dropped, the preceding vowel becomes short. Examples:

> hate (long *a*)   hat (short *a*)
> dine (long *i*)   din (short *i*)

Thus the terminal silent *e* is usually at work. However, because of the long-vowel, short-vowel principle *any* vowel will do the work of the silent *e,* for a vowel-consonant-vowel sequence would still be maintained, making the first vowel long if it is in an accented syllable. Thus when a suffix beginning with a vowel is added to a word ending in a silent *e,* the silent *e* is no longer needed because the vowel of the suffix will do the work of the silent *e,* which therefore can be dropped. Hence we have the basic silent *e* rule.

    Here are examples of the rule in action:

> dine + ing = dining
> write + ing = writing
> guide + ance = guidance
> mange + y = mangy
> condole + ence = condolence
> bite + ing = biting
> shine + ing = shining
> interfere + ed = interfered
> create + ive = creative

shine + y = shiny
fame + ous = famous
confuse + ing = confusing

In words like these the long-vowel sound is preserved because a vowel-consonant-vowel sequence is maintained.

Some words in English, however, end in silent *e*'s that do no work, but the rule still applies to them. Examples:

come + ing = coming
hypocrite + ical = hypocritical
imagine + ative = imaginative
pursue + ing = pursuing

The silent *e*'s in these words do not make the preceding vowels long; they are just part of the many irregularities in English spelling. Still, the basic rule applies to them.

15C THE RETENTION-OF-THE-SILENT-E RULES

There are two rules for retaining silent *e*'s when suffixes are added. The first is an important exception to the basic rule in the previous section.

<u>Rule 3</u> **When adding the suffix *able, ous,* or *ance* to a word that ends in a silent e preceded by a c or g, retain the silent e.**

This rule, too, is based on important phonetic principles in English spelling. Both the *c* and the *g* are used for spelling two entirely different sounds.* First we will consider the *c,* which (with a few exceptions) is pronounced either as an *s,* as in *city,* or as a *k,* as in *cable.* The *c* pronounced as an *s* is called a soft *c,* and the *c* pronounced

---

* In addition the *c* has a *ch* sound in some imported words, such as *cello* and *concerto,* and is silent in some other words, such as *indict* and *muscle. Ch* is a single sound unlike the usual sounds *c* stands for. Also, there are some complex aspects of *g* that we will not explain, for they are not involved in the rule we are discussing.

as a *k* is called a hard *c*. A *c* is almost always soft when it is followed by an *e, i,* or *y,* and it is almost always hard when it is followed by an *a, o,* or *u* or when it is the last letter of a word or syllable. Thus when a word ends in a silent *e* preceded by a *c,* the silent *e* is doing the job of making the *c* soft. For example, the *c* is soft in *service,* but if the silent *e* is dropped, we would pronounce the remainder *ser-vik.* Similarly, if when adding the suffix *able* to *service* we dropped the silent *e,* the *c* would be followed by an *a,* thus becoming hard, and we would have the pronunciation *ser-vik-able.* Since we want the pronunciation *ser-viss-able,* we retain the silent *e* so that the *c* will remain soft.

For convenience, here is a repetition of this part of the general rule:

When adding *able* to a word that ends in a silent e preceded by a *c*, retain the silent e to preserve the soft *c* sound.

Here are typical examples:

    replace + able = replaceable
    notice + able = noticeable
    trace + able = traceable
    splice + able = spliceable
    peace + able = peaceable
    embrace + able = embraceable

Another rule involving the hard *c* is this:

When adding the suffix y or a suffix beginning with e or i to a word that ends in c, add a k in order to preserve the hard *c* sound.

For example, if the suffix *ed* were added to the verb *panic,* the *c* would become soft and produce the pronunciation *pan-iced.* So we add a *k* to preserve the hard *c* sound. Here are examples of the main words involved in this minor rule:

    panic + ed = panicked   picnic + ing = picnicking
    panic + y = panicky   politic + ing = politicking
    picnic + er = picnicker   traffic + ing = trafficking

Many of our words already have the *k*, such as *kick* and *pick*.

Now we will consider the *g*. The hard *g* is pronounced *guh*, as in *got* and *begin*. The soft *g* is pronounced as a *j*, as in *gin* and *gyp*. The two sounds of *g* do not follow regular phonetic principles to the extent that the two sounds of *c* do, for the *g* is sometimes soft and sometimes hard when followed by *e* or *i*. However, the *g* is virtually always soft when followed by a silent *e* and virtually always hard when followed by *a, o,* or *u* or when it is the final letter of a word. Thus we have this part of the general rule:

> **When adding *able, ous,* or *ance* to a word ending in a silent *e* preceded by a *g*, retain the silent *e* to preserve the soft *g* sound.**

For example, *arrange* has a soft *g*. But if when adding *able* to *arrange* we dropped the silent *e*, the pronunciation would be *ar-rang-able*. Thus we keep the silent *e* to preserve the soft *g* sound: *ar-range-able.* Here are other examples:

    courage + ous = courageous
    outrage + ous = outrageous
    advantage + ous = advantageous
    stage + able = stageable
    charge + able = chargeable
    change + able = changeable

Now the second rule for retention of the silent *e:*

Rule 4   **When adding a suffix beginning with a consonant to a word ending in a silent *e*, retain the silent *e*.**

The long-vowel, short-vowel principle makes this rule necessary. For example, the silent *e* in *fate* makes the *a* long. If the silent *e* were dropped when the suffix *ful* is added, the pronunciation would be *fat-ful.* Here are other examples of the rule in action:

    like + ness = likeness   hate + ful = hateful
    late + ly = lately   safe + ty = safety
    complete + ly = completely   care + less = careless

The *e* must be retained to prevent such pronunciations as *lik-ness* and *lat-ly*.

Sometimes the final silent *e* does not make the preceding vowel long, but the rule still holds. Examples:

immediate + ly = immediately
appropriate + ly = appropriately
approximate + ly = approximately
delicate + ly = delicately

Misspellings due to the dropping of the silent *e* when adding *ly* are quite common.

There are a few exceptions to the above rule. Here are the main ones:

whole + ly = wholly   argue + ment = argument
true + ly = truly   judge + ment = judgment
awe + ful = awful

In these words the silent *e* is dropped even though the suffix added begins with a consonant.

15D   THE Y-TO-*I* RULE

<u>Rule 5</u> **When adding a suffix to a word ending in y preceded by a consonant, change the y to *i*. If the y is preceded by a vowel, do not change the y to *i*.**

When adding the suffix *s* to make the plural of a noun that ends in *y* preceded by a consonant or when adding the suffix *s* to a verb that ends in *y* preceded by a consonant, change the *y* to *i* and add *es*. Examples:

ally + s = allies   try + s = tries
reply + s = replies   deny + s = denies
harpy + s = harpies   defy + s = defies

The rule also operates with many other suffixes. Examples:

comply + ance = compliance   cry + er = crier
mercy + ful = merciful   dry + est = driest
lonely + ness = loneliness   easy + ly = easily

The rule does not apply when the suffix is *ing* or *ist.*
Examples:

study + ing = studying	worry + ing = worrying
hurry + ing = hurrying	copy + ist = copyist

In these words the *y* is *never* dropped; misspellings such as *studing* for *studying* are common.

There are a number of exceptions to the rule, all of them involving one-syllable words. Here are the main exceptions:

shyness	slyly	dryness
shyly	wryness	dryly
slyness	wryly	dryer (the machine)

A minor rule that reverses the *y-to-i* rule is this:

When adding *ing* to a verb ending in *ie*, change the *ie* to *y.*

Examples:

die + ing = dying	tie + ing = tying
lie + ing = lying	vie + ing = vying

For convenience, here is a repetition of the second part of the y-to-i rule:

When adding a suffix to a word ending in *y* preceded by a vowel, do not change the *y* to *i.*

Examples:

annoy + s = annoys	valley + s = valleys
convey + ed = conveyed	alley + s = alleys
stay + ed = stayed	donkey + s = donkeys
coy + ly = coyly	boy + hood = boyhood

There are a few common exceptions to this part of the rule:

lay + ed = laid	day + ly = daily
pay + ed = paid	gay + ly = gaily
say + ed = said	

In these words the *y* is changed to *i* even though the *y* is preceded by a vowel.

The y-to-i rule does not apply in spelling the plural of proper names nor the possessive form of any noun ending in *y.* Examples:

the Bradys	Betty's car
the Kennedys	one ally's advantage
several Sallys	the company's president

15E THE *IE/EI* RULES

The *ie/ei* rules do not cover many words, but they do cover common words that are frequently misspelled.

<u>Rule 6</u> **Place *i* before *e* when pronounced as *ee* except after *c*. Place *e* before *i* after *c*.**

Most Important: This rule covers only *ie* or *ei* combinations that are pronounced as the single long *e* sound. That is, the rule does not apply to such words as *science* and *atheist,* in which the *i*'s and *e*'s are pronounced in separate syllables, or to such words as *foreign* and *friend,* in which the combination is not pronounced as a long *o.*

To spell correctly with this rule you must know everything about a word except whether it has an *ie* or *ei* combination. For example, if you don't know that *receipt* has a silent *p,* you can apply the rule correctly and still misspell the word. Here are some common words covered by the rule:

believe	receive
chief	deceive
achieve	deceit
priest	conceive
thief	conceit
brief	receipt
relieve	ceiling
yield	perceive
niece	
tier	
mien	

There are a number of exceptions to this rule, but the only ones that give any trouble can be mastered by memorizing this nonsense sentence:

Neither sheik seized weird leisure.

All five of these exceptions have an *ei* combination pronounced as a long *e* but not preceded by a *c*. (In some dialects *neither* is pronounced with a long *i* sound and *leisure* with an *eh* sound.)

Rule 7 **Place *e* before *i* when pronounced as a long *a*.**

Of course there are various ways of spelling the long *a* sound, but if the word has either an *ie* or *ei* combination, then the writer can know that it is *ei* if the pronunciation is a long *a*. Here are some common words covered by this rule:

freight	reins
weight	vein
neighbor	neigh
sleigh	reign
heinous	deign

The words *their* and *heir* may also be put in this group, though the vowel sound in them is not exactly a long *a* in many people's dialects.

16

Spelling Lists

16A DOUBLE-CONSONANT WORDS

The following words are often misspelled because one consonant of a double consonant is omitted. The double consonants are in boldface.

ac**c**idental	begi**nn**er	embar**ra**ss
ac**c**ommodate	begi**nn**ing	equi**pp**ed
ac**c**omplish	bi**gg**est	exa**gg**erate
ac**c**urate	co**mm**ittee	exce**ll**ent
a**gg**ressive	co**mm**unist	genera**ll**y
a**nn**ual	contro**ll**ed	i**mm**ediately
a**pp**aratus	curriculum	i**mm**ense
a**pp**arent	di**ff**erent	inte**ll**igence
a**pp**lies	disa**pp**ear	inte**ll**igent
a**pp**reciate	disa**pp**oint	inter**r**upt
a**pp**ropriate	di**ss**atisfied	ir**r**itable
a**pp**roximate	di**ss**ervice	ma**nn**er
a**tt**itude	drunke**nn**ess	mi**ss**pelled

narrative	planned	success
necessary	possess	summed
occurred	possession	supposed
occurrence	possible	suppress
opponent	preferred	surrounding
opportunity	roommate	swimming
opposite	stubborn	unnecessary
parallel		

16B SINGLE-CONSONANT WORDS

The following words are often misspelled because a single consonant is incorrectly doubled. The single consonant is in boldface.

abandoned	disappoint
academic	during
across	eliminate
already	fulfill
among	holiday
amount	imagine
analyze	inoculate
another	interfered
apartment	later
apology	necessary
becoming	occasion
benefited	omitted
biting	operate
calendar	opinion
career	parallel
column	primitive
coming	profession
confused	professor
define	quarrel
definitely	relative
definition	shining
dining	tomorrow
disappear	writing

16C *DE* AND *DI* WORDS

The following words are often misspelled because an *e* is substituted for an *i* or an *i* for an *e*. The *de*'s and *di*'s are in boldface.

descend	**di**gest
describe	**di**gress
description	**di**lemma
despair	**di**lute
despise	**di**sastrous
despite	**di**sciple
destroy	**di**sease
destruction	**di**vide
device	**di**vine
devise	**di**vorce

16D OMITTED LETTERS

The following words are often misspelled because of the omission of one or more letters. The letters that are often omitted are in boldface.

acci**d**ent**all**y	char**ac**teristics	fami**l**y
accompany**i**ng	cloth**es**	fas**c**inate
a**c**quire	(two) communist**s**	four**t**h
advertis**e**ment	compe**ti**tion	gover**n**ment
appropriat**e**ly	complet**e**ly	hero**es**
approximat**e**ly	(it) consist**s**	hope**l**ess
as**p**irin	criti**c**ism	hypocrit**e**
ath**e**ist	crowd**e**d	imagin**e**
basical**l**y	dealt	immediat**e**ly
barg**ai**n	definit**e**ly	inter**e**st
befor**e**	dis**c**ipline	knowled**g**e
bound**a**ry	envir**o**nment	lab**o**ratory
car**e**less	every**t**hing	lik**e**ly
carry**i**ng	experi**e**nce	litera**t**ure
chang**e**able	extrem**e**ly	

loneliness	(be) prejudiced	studying
lonely	primitive	supposed (to)
luxury	privilege	temperament
magazine	probably	temperature
mathematics	quantity	therefore
meant	realize	thorough
medical	remember	undoubtedly
medicine	rhythm	used (to)
Negroes	safety	useful
ninety	(two) scientists	valuable
noticeable	shepherd	various
nowadays	sincerely	where
numerous	sophomore	whether
particular	stretch	whose

16E ADDED LETTERS

The following words are often misspelled because of the addition of a letter. The incorrect letters that are often added are in parentheses. (Also see Section 16B.)

among (no *u* after *o*)
argument (no *e* after *u*)
athlete (no *e* after *h*)
attack (no *t* after *k*)
awful (no *e* after *w*)
chosen (no *oo*)
disastrous (no *e* after *t*)
drowned (no *d* after *n*)
equipment (no *t* after *p*)
exercise (no *c* after *x*)
existent (no *h* after *x*)
explanation (no *i* after *la*)
final (no *i* after *n*)
forty (no *u* after *o*)
forward (no *e* after *r*)
genius (no *o* after *i*)
grievous (no *i* after *v*)

height (no *h* after *t*)
Henry (no *e* after *n*)
hindrance (no *e* after *d*)
jewelry (no *e* after *l*)
judgment (no *e* after *g*)
laundry (no *e* after *d*)
led (no *a* after *e*)
lose (no *oo*)
mischievous (no *i* after *v*)
ninth (no *e* after *in*)
pamphlet (no *e* after *h*)
personal (no *i* after *n*)
privilege (no *d* after *le*)
procedure (no *ee*)
remembrance (no *e* after *b*)
similar (no *i* after *l*)
statistics (no *s* after *a*)
truly (no *e* after *u*)

16F *ANT-ANCE* AND *ENT-ENCE* WORDS

abund**ant**	resist**ant**	exist**ence**
abund**ance**	resist**ance**	experi**ence**
acquaint**ance**	serv**ant**	independ**ent**
admitt**ance**	warr**ant**	independ**ence**
appear**ance**		ingredi**ent**
assist**ant**	abs**ent**	insist**ent**
assist**ance**	abs**ence**	insist**ence**
attend**ant**	adolesc**ent**	intellig**ent**
attend**ance**	adolesc**ence**	intellig**ence**
brilli**ant**	appar**ent**	magnific**ent**
brilli**ance**	coher**ent**	magnific**ence**
const**ant**	coher**ence**	occurr**ence**
domin**ant**	compet**ent**	oppon**ent**
domin**ance**	compet**ence**	perman**ent**
guid**ance**	confid**ent**	perman**ence**
hindr**ance**	confid**ence**	persist**ent**
ignor**ant**	consist**ent**	persist**ence**
ignor**ance**	consist**ence**	pres**ent**
import**ant**	conveni**ent**	pres**ence**
import**ance**	conveni**ence**	promin**ent**
inhabit**ant**	depend**ent**	promin**ence**
pleas**ant**	depend**ence**	rever**ent**
predomin**ant**	differ**ent**	rever**ence**
redund**ant**	differ**ence**	suffici**ent**
redund**ance**	excell**ent**	suffici**ence**
relev**ant**	excell**ence**	superintend**ent**
relev**ance**	exist**ent**	superintend**ence**

16G HOMOPHONES AND CONFUSED WORDS

Homophones are words that are pronounced alike but
that have different spellings and meanings, such as
course and *coarse.* The following list consists of homophones that cause frequent misspellings and also other

pairs of words which are so similar that the spelling of one is often confused with the spelling of the other. Information about the words is also included. The abbreviations used have the following meanings: n. = noun; v. = verb; adj. = adjective;   adv. = adverb;   pro. = pronoun; prep. = preposition; conj. = conjunction; poss. = possessive; contr. = contraction; sing. = singular; and pl. = plural.

accept: (v.) to receive
except: (prep.) not included

access: (n.) a way of approach or entrance
assess: (v.) to estimate the value of

adapt: (v.) to adjust to a situation
adopt: (v.) to take in or take a course of action

advice: (n.) counsel, information, or suggestions given
advise: (v.) to give advice or counsel

affect: (v.) to influence or have an effect on
effect: (n.) the result of an action
effect: (v.) to accomplish or execute

aisle: (n.) a corridor or passageway
isle: (n.) an island

all ready: (n. + adj.) everyone is prepared
already: (adv.) at or before this time; previously

all together: (n. + adj.) all in one place
altogether: (adv.) completely; wholly

allude: (v.) to refer to
elude: (v.) to evade or escape

allusion: (n.) a reference
illusion: (n.) a false impression

aloud: (adv.) audibly or loudly
allowed: (v.) permitted

altar: (n.) an elevated place for religious services
alter: (v.) to change

always: (adv.) constantly; all the time
all ways: (determiner + n.) in every way

anecdote: (n.) a little story
antidote: (n.) something that counteracts a poison

angel: (n.) a heavenly being
angle: (n.) figure formed by the divergence of two straight lines from a common point

arc: (n.) a part of a circle
arch: (n.) a curved part of a building

ascend: (v.) to rise or go up
ascent: (n.) a movement upward
assent: (v.) to agree
assent: (n.) an agreement

assistance: (n.) help given
assistants: (n. pl.) helpers

band: (n.) a group
banned: (v.) excluded or prohibited

beside: (prep.) by the side of
besides: (adv. *and* prep.) in addition to

boar: (n.) a male hog
bore: (n.) someone who tires you

boarder: (n.) one who pays for room and meals
border: (n.) a boundary

born: (v.) given birth to (always in the passive voice)
borne: (v.) given birth to (always in the active voice); carried

brake: (n.) a mechanism to stop a vehicle
break: (v.) to cause to fall into two or more pieces

breath: (n.) air inhaled and exhaled
breathe: (v.) to take in breaths and let them out

canvas: (n.) a kind of coarse cloth
canvass: (v.) to search or examine or solicit

capital: (n.) a city that is a seat of government
capitol: (n.) a building occupied by a legislature

censer: (n.) container for burning incense
censor: (v.) to prohibit publication
censor: (n.) one who prohibits publication
censure: (v.) to reprimand or disapprove of
censure: (n.) disapproval

choose: (v.) to select (present tense)
chose: (v.) selected (past tense)
chosen: (v.) selected (past participle)

cite: (v.) to quote; to charge with breaking a law
sight: (n.) something seen; the sense of seeing
sight: (v.) to look at or aim at
site: (n.) a location

coarse: (adj.) rough; unrefined
course: (n.) school subject; a way or path

complement: (n.) items which complete
compliment: (n.) a statement of praise

conscience: (n.) what tells you right from wrong
conscious: (adj.) awake; alert

council: (n.) a group that deliberates
counsel: (v.) to give advice
counsel: (n.) advice given

descent: (n.) a going down
dissent: (v.) to disagree
dissent: (n.) disagreement

desert: (n.) a geographical area
desert: (v.) to abandon
dessert: (n.) food

device: (n.) a contrivance
devise: (v.) to prepare a method or contrivance

do: (v.) to perform
due: (adj.) used with *to* to specify the cause of something; owing

dual: (adj.) twofold
duel: (n.) a fight between two people

eminent: (adj.) famous
imminent: (adj.) likely to occur soon

envelop: (v.) to cover or enclose
envelope: (n.) an enclosure used for mailing

extant: (adj.) still existing
extent: (n.) the degree of something

formally: (adv.) in a formal manner
formerly: (adv.) at an earlier time

forth: (adv., prep.) forward; onward; out
fourth: (n.) the one after the third

human: (adj.) pertaining to people
humane: (adj.) pertaining to compassion or kindness

its: (poss. pro.) belonging to it
it's: (contr.) it is *or* it has

later: (adj.) after a specified time
latter: (n.) the last one mentioned

lead: (v.; pronounced *leed*) to conduct
lead: (n.; pronounced *led*) the metal
led: (v.) past tense and past participle of the verb *lead*

loose: (adj.) not tight
lose: (v.) to misplace; to be defeated

marital: (adj.) pertaining to marriage
martial: (adj.) military

maybe: (adv.) perhaps
may be: (v.) possibly may occur

meant: (v.) past tense and past participle of the verb
mean
ment: not a word

passed: (v.) past tense and past participle of the verb
pass

past: (n.) an earlier time

patience: (sing. n.) calm endurance
patients: (pl. n.) those under medical care

peace: (n.) not war
piece: (n.) a part of

personal: (adj.) pertaining to oneself
personnel: (n.) the employees of a company or organization

principal: (n.) head of a school; money owned
principal: (adj.) chief; most important
principle: (n.) a rule or doctrine

prophecy: (n.) a prediction
prophesy: (v.) to make a prediction

quiet: (adj.) not noisy
quite: (adv.) completely or almost completely

sense: (n.) ability to think well; meaning
since: (prep. *and* conj.) before this time; because

stationary: (adj.) in a fixed position
stationery: (n.) paper to write on

than: (conj.) used to compare things
then: (n. or adv.) indicating time

their: (poss. pro.) belonging to them
there: (adv.) a place; also used as an expletive to begin sentences
they're: (contr.) they are

to: (prep.) generally indicating direction
too: (adv.) excessively; overmuch
two: (n.) the number

trail: (n.) a rough path
trial: (n.) experimental action, or examination before a court

vice: (n.) immorality
vise: (n.) a device for holding

weather: (n.) the state of the atmosphere
whether: (conj.) expressing alternatives

whose: (poss. pro.) belonging to whom
who's: (contr.) who is *or* who has

your: (poss. pro.) belonging to you
you're: (contr.) you are

16H OTHER TROUBLESOME WORDS

The following common words, not included in the preceding sections, are also often misspelled.

a lot	eighth	nickel	schedule
actually	endeavor	optimism	separate
against	familiar	ours	sergeant
amateur	favorite	paid	source
amount	February	peculiar	speech
article	foreign	perspiration	supersede
battalion	grammar	practical	surprise
beauty	guarantee	precede	technique
bulletin	hers	preparation	theirs
buried	hundred	prescription	themselves
category	inevitable	prestige	tragedy
children	interpretation	proceed	Tuesday
comparative	involve	psychology	until
condemn	January	pursue	Wednesday
counselor	library	repetition	(one) woman
courtesy	marriage	ridiculous	yours
doesn't	minute	sacrifice	

Note: A proper name ending in *y* is made plural by the
addition of *s* (the Darbys) and a name ending in *s* is made
plural by the addition of *es,* with no apostrophe (the
Davis*es*).

17

Capitalization

Although practices in capitalization do vary, the following specific rules are adhered to by almost all writers. The name commonly used for small letters is **lower case.**

17A RULES OF CAPITALIZATION

For convenience, we will not only use our number-letter system of classification but also will number the rules.

17A1 The Basics

<u>Rule 1</u> **Capitalize the first word of each sentence, the pronoun *I*, and the interjection *O*, but not other interjections unless one opens a sentence. In using direct quotations, follow the capitalization of the original author exactly.**

17A2 Titles of Literary Works

Rule 2 **In a title or chapter heading, capitalize the first word and all other words except articles, short prepositions, and coordinating conjunctions.**

Examples:

TITLE OF A BOOK: *The Decline and Fall of the Roman Empire*
TITLE OF A SHORT STORY: "The Capital of the World"
TITLE OF A POEM: "The Death of the Hired Man"
CHAPTER HEADING: The Debate Between Skinner and Foster

17A3 Specific School Courses

Rule 3 **Capitalize the name of a specific school course but not the name of a general subject-matter area, unless it is a proper name.**

Examples:

I am taking History 17A and American Literature Since 1865, but I would rather be taking courses in chemistry and math.

17A4 Proper Nouns and Proper Adjectives

Rule 4 **Capitalize all proper nouns and adjectives formed from proper nouns, unless the proper adjective—such as *venetian red*—is commonly spelled with a lower-case letter.**

Consult a dictionary if necessary. A proper noun is the name of an individual of some sort, animate or inanimate. Examples:

Arabian	Mount Rushmore	San Franciscan
English	Newtonian	Statue of Liberty
French	New Yorker	Sweden
Hollywoodish	Oriental	Swedish
John Doe	Platonism	Yosemite

17A5   Religions and Related Topics

Rule 5   Capitalize references to the Deity or Deities in all recognized religions, the names of religions, religious sects, divine books, and adjectives formed from these.

Examples:

Allah	Christ	our Lord
Baptist	Christian	Mormonism
the Bible	God	the New Testament
Biblical	Hinduism	Protestant
Catholic	Jewish	the Upanishads

17A6   Relatives

Rule 6   Capitalize the titles of relatives when used with the person's name or as a substitute for the name, but not when the term designating the relationship is used with a possessive pronoun, such as *my*.

Examples:

The caller was Aunt Helen.
The caller was my aunt Helen.
My mother is a nurse.
Did Mother say it was all right?
We see Grandfather Brown playing golf daily.

Usage varies with terms of relationship used as names in direct address.

"Thanks for the help, son (*or* Son)."
"Tell me again, Father (or father), how you won."

17A7   Officials

Rule 7   Capitalize the titles of important officials when used with their names. Capitalize a title used in place of a name to designate a particular individual.

Do not capitalize a title that designates an office but not a particular individual.

Examples:

> Vice-President Forbes
> Senator Javits
> Colonel Wetzler
> Reverend Puder
> The Congressman will not be in today. (A specific congressman is understood.)
> The Dean left instructions for preparing the memo. (A specific dean is understood.)
> A college president does not have an enviable job. (No specific president is meant.)
> The office of mayor is vacant.

17A8 Days, Months, and Holidays

Rule 8   **Capitalize the days of the week, the months of the year, and official holidays. Do not capitalize the names of the seasons.**

Examples:

Admission Day	February	Wednesday
Christmas	Veterans Day	winter

17A9 Specific Geographic Locations

Rule 9   **Capitalize the names of nations, states, provinces, continents, oceans, lakes, rivers, mountains, cities, streets, parks, and specific geographic regions. Do not capitalize the names of directions.**

Examples:

Alabama	Jefferson Park	the South
Alberta	Lake Louise	Tenth Street
Asia	the Near East	Uganda
Baltimore	the Pacific Ocean	Walk east two blocks.
Deer Mountain	the Red River	the West Coast

17A10   Buildings

Rule 10   **Capitalize the names of specific buildings.**

Badgley **S**cience **H**all   the **P**alace **T**heater
the **H**aberfeld **B**uilding   the **P**entagon

17A11   Private and Governmental Organizations

Rule 11   **Capitalize the names of private and governmental organizations.**

Examples:

the **A**merican **L**egion   **R**otary
the **E**lks **C**lub   the **S**tate **D**epartment
the **P**eace **C**orps   the **V**eterans **A**dministration

17A12   Historical Documents, Events, and Eras

Rule 12   **Capitalize the names of historical documents, events, and eras.**

Examples:

the **A**tlantic **C**harter   the **M**iddle **A**ges
the **B**attle of **M**idway   **P**ublic **L**aw 16
the **B**ill of **R**ights   the **R**enaissance
the **D**iet of **W**orms   **W**orld **W**ar II

17A13   Brand Names

Rule 13   **Capitalize brand names but not the name of
the product.**

Examples:

Arco gasoline   a **F**ord car
Dial soap   **M**um deodorant

17A14 Outline Headings

<u>Rule 14</u> **Capitalize the first word of an outline heading.**

Examples:

    I. Uses of the dictionary
      A. To determine multiple definitions of a particular word
        1. Methods of ordering definitions
          a. By frequency of use

17A15 Celestial Bodies

<u>Rule 15</u> **Capitalize the names of celestial bodies and of geographic regions of the moon.**

Do not capitalize the words *earth, world, universe, galaxy, moon,* and *sun.* Examples:

Arcturus (a star)	Phobos (a moon of Mars)
the Crab Nebula	the Sea of Rains (on the moon)
Halley's Comet	Venus

Exception: When named as a planet among other planets, *earth* is generally capitalized.

In the solar system, Earth is between Venus and Mars.

17A16 Abbreviations

<u>Rule 16</u> **Capitalize abbreviations when the whole word or phrase would be capitalized.**

See Section 14C for other aspects of the capitalization of abbreviations and also for punctuation in abbreviations. Examples:

b. 1891 (born)	the **NAACP**
CORE	Oct.
120 **h.p.** (horsepower)	the **UN**
gloss. (glossary)	the **U.S.** Army

17B MANDATORY LOWER-CASE LETTERS

17B1 Centuries

<u>Rule 17</u> **Do not capitalize the names of centuries unless a century is being mentioned as a specific historical era.**

Examples:

> It was my destiny to be born in the twentieth century.
> The Age of the Enlightenment is sometimes called simply the Eighteenth Century.

17B2 Common Animate and Inanimate Objects

<u>Rule 18</u> **Do not capitalize the names of foods, games, chemical compounds, general geographical formations, animals, plants, or musical instruments unless they designate specific individuals or kinds.**

Sometimes, however, a proper noun, which is capitalized, is a part of the name of a species. Examples:

> a Baltimore oriole
> bridge
> a Canary pine
> canyon
> our cat, Princess
> collie
> escarpment
> a game of Scrabble
> golf
> Lady Baltimore cake
> maple
> piano
> rice
> robin
> rose
> schist
> spaghetti

sulfur dioxide
Thompson's gazelle
trout
violoncello

17B3 Occupations

<u>Rule 19</u>   **Do not capitalize the names of occupations.**

Examples:

doctor
engineer
professor

17B4 Diseases

<u>Rule 20</u>   **Do not capitalize the names of diseases.**

Sometimes, however, a proper noun, which is capitalized, is part of the name of the disease. Examples:

gastritis
Hodgkin's disease
mumps

18

The Apostrophe

The apostrophe is a mark used in spelling, not a mark of punctuation. Marks of punctuation clarify sentence structure, whereas apostrophes clarify word form.

18A THE APOSTROPHE IN POSSESSIVE CONSTRUCTIONS

There are two ways of expressing possession in English (aside from simply saying *I own something*). The one is to use *belonging to* or an *of*-construction, as in *the good looks of Estella* or *the power of the President.* The more common is with the so-called possessive construction in which the person or thing doing the possessing comes in front of the thing possessed, as in *Estella's good looks* or *the President's power.*

18A1   Possessive Nouns

Use an apostrophe with a common or a proper noun in a possessive construction.

Spoken English simply adds an *s*-like sound to a noun that shows some idea of possession. Written English is not quite that simple; in addition to the *s*, it requires placing an apostrophe correctly (either before or after the *s*, never directly above it). **Singular nouns always add the apostrophe first and then the letter *s* to form the possessive case.**

> Gilbert**'s** toys = toys belonging to Gilbert
> Betty**'s** nose = the nose of Betty
> Shakespeare**'s** plays = plays Shakespeare wrote
>   the table**'s** legs = legs of the table

Even when the base form of the noun already ends in *s*, add both the apostrophe as well as another *s* to form the possessive (though some writers add only the apostrophe).

> a waitress**'s** tips *or* a waitress**'** tips
> Chris**'s** comments *or* Chris**'** comments

Most nouns form their plurals by adding *s* or *es;* a few do not (man, men; woman, women; child, children; fish, fish; sheep, sheep; goose, geese; mouse, mice). When a plural noun shows possession, **always form the plural first and then add the mark of possession.** If the plural of a noun ends in *s*, add only the apostrophe.

> boys**'** caps = caps belonging to several boys
> students**'** habits = habits of a number of students
> many houses**'** roofs = roofs of many houses

If the plural of a noun does not end in *s*, add both the apostrophe and an *s* in that order.

> men**'s** suits = suits of many men
> women**'s** activities = activities of many women
> children**'s** toys = toys of a number of children
> mice**'s** nests = nests of several mice

In writing, do not confuse the simple plural with the possessive plural—though in speech they may sound alike. For example, if the parents of children of a family named Goss were to come to your house, you would write the following:

> The Gosses came. (no apostrophe)

But if their car stalled on the way, you would use an apostrophe, as follows:

> The Gosses' car stalled.

Such a construction would indicate both the plural (by the *es*) and possession (by the apostrophe).

Sometimes a possessive noun ends a sentence, and the thing possessed is understood though not named. Such a possessive noun takes an apostrophe.

> Carol's baby weighs more than Jane**'s.**
> My stereo cost more than Betty**'s.**

18A2   Possessive Personal Pronouns

Do not use an apostrophe with a personal pronoun in a possessive construction.

Personal pronouns (see Section 1A5f) may have two possessive forms. Use the first form when a noun follows.

> These are **our** seats.
> Do you have **your** tickets?
> Jane made **her** blouse.

Use the second form when the following noun is understood. Note, however, that the possessives of personal pronouns never take an apostrophe.

> They had already found their seats, but we were still looking
>   for **ours.** (no apostrophe)
> I paid $7.00 for my ticket; how much was **yours?** (no apostrophe)
> Dottie bought her blouse at a boutique, but Jane made **hers.**
>   (no apostrophe)

Distinguish between *its* (belonging to *it*) and *it's* (contraction of *it is*).

RIGHT: **It's** (= it is) too hot to work today.
RIGHT: My car runs fine but **its** muffler (= belonging to it) is shot.

18A3 Possessive Indefinite Pronouns

Use an apostrophe with an indefinite pronoun in a possessive construction.

A group of words called **indefinite pronouns** function as nouns and may be called noun substitutes. The chief ones that can be made possessive are *one, no one, someone, anyone, everyone, somebody, anybody, everybody, nobody, other, another, one another,* and *each other.* Also the *one* and *body* words are often used with *else,* as in *somebody else.* When one of these words is in a possessive construction, it requires an apostrophe and an *s.* Since none of these words ends in *s,* the apostrophe will always come before the *s.* Examples:

RIGHT: Somebody**'s** nose is going to be bloodied if it gets closer to me.
I couldn't think of anyone**'s** phone number.
Everybody else**'s** habits need reforming.
We should all be concerned with each other**'s** welfare.

You can put it into your mind that anytime you hear the *s* on one of the *one* or *body* words (except *one* itself) or on the *else,* the spelling will virtually always be *'s.*

18A4 Possessive Nouns That Name Periods of Time and Sums of Money

Use an apostrophe to show a possessive construction with a period of time or a sum of money.

Words that name periods of time are frequently used in possessive construction in English, and they take apostrophes just as any other nouns do. Examples:

RIGHT: One month's vacation is preferable to two months' salary.
       Today's crisis is no worse than yesterday's.
       February's weather made me think the year's death was occurring.
       An hour's value nowadays seems to be $14, at least for plumbers.

Words that name sums of money are also used in the possessive construction in English and require apostrophes just as other nouns do. Examples:

RIGHT: One dollar's worth of steak won't register on the scales.
       I prefer a quarter's worth of gin to two dollars' worth of cola.
       There wasn't a nickel's difference in our tallies.
       Your two cents' worth will get you nowhere.

18B THE APOSTROPHE IN CONTRACTIONS

Use an apostrophe in a contraction.

In contractions, enter an apostrophe where one or more letters have been omitted. Examples:

don't	shouldn't (not should'nt)
doesn't (not does'nt)	o'clock
we've	I'm
you'll	Henry's here.
they're	Everybody's gone.

Do *not* confuse contractions with personal possessive pronouns. The possessive pronouns are already possessive, and so nothing else—not even an apostrophe—is needed to make them possessive. Examples:

possessive pronouns	*pronoun contractions*
its (belonging to it)	it's (it is *or* it has)
whose (belonging to whom)	who's (who is *or* who has)

<u>*possessive pronouns*</u>

your (belonging to you)
their (belonging to them)

<u>*pronoun contractions*</u>

you're (you are)
they're (they are)

Also, *never* put an apostrophe in one of these possessive pronouns:

yours   hers   ours   theirs

These words are already possessive, as *his* and *mine* are, and must not take an apostrophe.

18C THE APOSTROPHE IN PLURAL SPELLINGS

Use apostrophes in certain plural spellings.

Use an *'s* to form the plural of words used as words (see Section 14B, Rule 3 for underlining), of letters of the alphabet, of abbreviations, of numerals, and of symbols. Examples:

RIGHT: Don't put too many *if*'s in your proposal.
      There are four *s*'s and four *i*'s in *Mississippi.*
      Professor Smelly's capital *C*'s look like his *9*'s.
      Joey is more concerned with rpm's than with his girl-friend.
      The 1700's were good years for aristocrats.
      You have too many +'s in your equation.

The apostrophes in these plurals make for clarity. When there is no chance of the reader's being momentarily confused, some writers omit apostrophes in some of these special plural spellings.

Caution: Never spell the ordinary nonpossessive plural of a noun with an apostrophe. Examples:

WRONG: Too many cook's spoil the broth.
RIGHT: Too many cooks spoil the broth.

WRONG: Many cooks' are unsanitary.
RIGHT: Many cooks are unsanitary.

19

The Hyphen

Like the apostrophe, the hyphen is a mark used in spelling, not a mark of punctuation. It should not be confused with the dash (see Section 11A), which is a mark of punctuation twice as long as the hyphen.

19A WORD DIVISION AT THE END OF A LINE

<u>Rule 1</u> **When dividing a word at the end of a line, use a hyphen and divide only between syllables.**

Never divide a one-syllable word, such as *tw-elve* and *len-gth*. Do not divide a word so that a single letter is left at the end of one line or the beginning of another, such as *a-muse* and *shin-y*. When necessary, consult a dictionary for proper syllabication.

19B COMPOUND NUMBERS AND FRACTIONS

<u>Rule 2</u> **Hyphenate spelled-out compound numbers (twenty-one through ninety-nine) and spelled-out fractions.**

If a fraction is unambiguously used with the indefinite article *a* or *an*, do not hyphenate it. Examples:

thirty-eight wins	two-fifths of my whisky
ninety-two losses	one-half of a loaf
our fifty-seventh anniversary	a third of the profits

Caution: Do *not* hyphenate noncompound numbers. Examples:

WRONG: one-hundred, three-thousand
RIGHT: one hundred, three thousand

Note that *twenty-four* really means twenty plus four but that *one hundred* does not mean one plus a hundred. It simply tells how many hundreds are involved.

19C COMPOUND NOUNS

<u>Rule 3</u> **Hyphenate compound nouns when hyphenation contributes to clarity.**

A compound noun is composed of two or more words that function as one noun. A few compound nouns—such as *son-in-law* and *self-control*—are always hyphenated, and some—such as *the White House* and *cooking apples*—never are. When necessary, consult a dictionary. Here are a few of the hyphenated compound nouns that appeared in one issue of a national magazine:

job-hunting	shadow-boxing
self-interest	kilowatt-hours
dry-goods	globe-trotters
well-being	by-product
Europe-firsters	passers-by

19D PREFIXES AND SUFFIXES

<u>Rule 4</u>   **Use a hyphen to separate the following pre-fixes and suffix from their root words: *self, all, ex* (meaning former), and *elect*.**

Examples:

> self-government for Togo
> an all-American quarterback
> an ex-mayor of Atlanta
> the governor-elect of Texas

Use a good dictionary to guide you in the use of such prefixes as *anti, co, non, pro, pseudo, quasi,* and *ultra.*

<u>Rule 5</u>   **Use a hyphen to separate a prefix when its last letter and the first letter of the root word are the same.**

Examples:

anti-industrial	de-emphasize
re-echo	pro-organization

Some common words, such as *cooperate,* do not now follow that rule. When necessary, consult a dictionary.

<u>Rule 6</u>   **Use a hyphen to separate a prefix when nonhyphenation might be ambiguous.**

Examples:

> a *co-op* and a *coop*
> to *re-collect* the equipment and to *recollect* a story
> to *re-cover* a sofa and to *recover* from an illness
> to *re-act* a scene and to *react* to a stimulant

<u>Rule 7</u>   **Use a hyphen to separate a prefix when the root word is capitalized.**

Examples:

non-Christian	mid-August
un-American	anti-Kennedy

19E COMPOUND ADJECTIVALS

<u>Rule 8</u> **Hyphenate two or more words that serve as a single adjectival in front of a noun.**

An adjectival is a modifier of a noun, and all kinds of English words can be combined to function as a single adjectival. Failure to hyphenate such adjectivals will often make a reader stumble momentarily or perhaps waste time figuring out word relationships. For example, this phrase appeared in a national advertisement:

The new embedded in plastic printed wiring circuit

Probably most readers had to pause to think out the word relationships, whereas if the writer had followed the above rule (plus the rule for separating coordinate adjectives) the meaning would have been immediately clear:

the new embedded-in-plastic, printed-wiring circuit

Rule 8 above is especially important for maintaining clarity in writing.

Here are some examples of Rule 8 taken from one issue of a national magazine:

cradle-to-grave needs	law-school faculty
two-fisted gesture	civil-rights battle
double-parked car	a soft-spoken type
all-too-human attributes	cigar-making firm
long-term outlay	an eight-year-old girl
state-supported schools	high-pressure steam

Long compound adjectivals should be hyphenated rather than enclosed in quotation marks. Example:

RIGHT: He took an I-won't-budge-an-inch-if-I-die attitude.

Note: Such adjectivals may correctly either precede or follow the nouns they modify. When they follow the noun, they are not normally hyphenated. Examples:

the law-school faculty	the faculty of a law school
all-too-human attributes	attributes that are all too human

an eight-year-old girl   a girl eight years old
a civil-rights battle   a battle for civil rights

__Rule 9__ **When a conjunction is entered into a compound adjectival so that two or more adjectivals are intended, leave a space before and after the conjunction but put a hyphen after the word or words that precede the conjunction.**

Examples:

all third- and fourth-grade pupils
all first-, second-, and third-ranked candidates

SECTION FOUR

DICTION

20

Appropriate Word Choice

Since writing takes many forms and fulfills many purposes, the words a writer chooses should be appropriate to the purpose. A great deal of slang might be appropriate in a friendly letter from one college student to another but quite inappropriate in a letter of application to be read by some unknown personnel officer. In discussing word choice (which is **diction**) in this chapter, we are limiting ourselves to the kind of writing usually called for in college—themes, essay exams, reports, and term papers.

Words wholly suitable for such kinds of writing may be classified into two groups: (1) **general-purpose words** and (2) **semiformal words.** General-purpose words are suitable for any writing situation and make up the bulk of most kinds of writing. They include virtually all the structure words, such as *no, some, about, such,* and *however,* and a great many common content words, such as *house, dress, sentence, hungry, good,* and *common.* Semiformal words are not commonly used in the casual conversation of people of moderate education, but they do occur frequently in semiformal or formal writing. Some examples are *disburse* (for *pay out*), *tortuous* (for *winding* or *twisting*), *subsequent* (for *coming after*), *rectitude* (for *moral behavior*), *rectify* (for *make right*), and *altruistic* (for *selfless* or *charitable*). Your college writing need not be limited exclusively to general-purpose and semiformal words, but you should be cautious in departing from these categories. The following sections give advice about appropriate word choice.

20A SLANG

Avoid using slang expressions.

Slang is language that seems to sprout from nowhere for the purpose of providing lively (and usually young) people with irreverent, racy, pungent, and sometimes off-color words and expressions to use instead of words that they consider stale or stuffy or inappropriate for their social situations. A typical example is *stop bugging me* for *stop annoying me.* Volumes could be written about slang, but the following points are sufficient for this chapter: (1) Slang is not bad language *per se;* it can be very good language when appropriately used. (2) The traditional four-letter obscenities and nonstandard words or constructions, such as *ain't got no,* are not slang. (3) A word—for example, *boogie-woogie*—is not slang unless it has a higher level counterpart in the language. (4) The distribution of slang terms both regionally and socially is extremely complex. (5) Some slang terms, such as *hang-up* and *burn artist,* are admirably effective coinages, but others, such as *lousy* and *peachy keen,* are so limp and colorless as to be offensive to anyone who loves language. (6) Most slang terms are new applications of established words, such as *burned out* for *exhausted,* but a few, such as *floozy* and *snafu,* are completely new coinages. (7) Most slang terms (even such as those in the examples below) are short-lived, for new generations are constantly rejecting some of the language of older people and inventing new slang terms for their own use. (8) Many slang terms, however, rise to the level of standard diction and thus enrich our vocabulary. *Freshman, tidy* (for *neat*), *club, tantrum, mob,* and many other common words were once scorned as mere slang. And (9) a few slang terms, such as *gab* (idle talk) and *guts* (courage), linger on as slang for centuries.

Since most of your writing for college classes (and later for the general public) is expository or argumentative, the general advice is to avoid slang. Though stated categorically, such advice is not absolute. If you consciously think that a pungent slang term will make your sentence more effective, use it without apology (but do not enclose it in quotation marks). Examples, with the slang terms in italics:

POOR STYLE: We had a real *blast* in Harvey's *pad* the other night, *rapping* until dawn.

EFFECTIVE USE OF SLANG: Within a day after agreeing to the partnership with Marlin, I realized I had a *pencilneck* on my hands and that the background in mechanics he boasted about was sheer *plastic.*

The ineffectiveness or effectiveness of a slang term can best be judged in the context of a whole paragraph or paper rather than in one sentence. Keep in mind, also, who your intended reader is. In general, slang—which appears occasionally in such high-level magazines as *Harper's* and *The Atlantic*—is most effective when it is sparingly used in conjunction with diction of a generally high level.

20B COLLOQUIALISMS

Use colloquial diction sparingly.

The word *colloquial* comes from a Latin word meaning "conversation." Originally, colloquial diction was considered suitable for informal conversation but not for writing.

Nowadays all but one of the good collegiate dictionaries use *informal* or *colloquial* to indicate that a word or one of its meanings is on a level below the semiformal.

Colloquial words are not necessarily to be avoided unless the situation is important enough to call for a higher level of diction. Levels of diction exist just as different modes of behavior exist in society. A bathrobe is suitable in a bedroom but would be out of place at a formal banquet. Similarly, *I have a bone to pick with you* might be acceptable in one situation, whereas *I have a disagreement to settle with you* might be appropriate for another situation. As a writer, you want to choose words that will do the most to improve your writing. For college writing, that means using colloquial diction judiciously.

Colloquial diction stretches from almost-slang to almost-semiformal. *To butter up* (to flatter) is barely above the slang level and normally would be inappropriate in semiformal writing; *to needle* (to goad or provoke) is close enough to the general-purpose category to pass without question in an article in a serious journal. Certain kinds of colloquial diction should be avoided in any writing of importance; much other colloquial diction has a secure place in writing as formal as a textbook. As you mature educationally, you will become more and more able to judge the levels of diction.

Here are some examples of colloquial diction in student writing, with semiformal revisions:

COLLOQUIAL: In algebra I was able to catch on without beating my brains out, and that made me feel a lot better about trying to go on in college.

SEMIFORMAL: I was able to understand algebra quite easily, and that encouraged me to continue my college studies.

COLLOQUIAL: When I thought she was giving me the eye, I got carried away and made a fool of myself by trying some shenanigans in the pool with her.

SEMIFORMAL: When I thought she was showing some interest in me, I overreacted and must have seemed foolish when I tried to get too friendly with her in the pool.

COLLOQUIAL: The boys thought they could get away with it by claiming over and over that they had told everything, but they couldn't bring it off.

SEMIFORMAL: The boys believed they could avoid their responsibility by claiming to be innocent, but they didn't succeed.

The colloquial sentences in these examples are *not* incorrect or even bad writing. However, the person whose writing vocabulary is limited to such a colloquial level will not be able to compose business letters, memos, and reports of the quality demanded in well-paying jobs of importance. So, though colloquial phrasing may work well in some situations, do not let it dominate your writing.

We should make two more points about colloquial diction. First, much colloquial diction in English consists of phrases that have single-word equivalents above the colloquial level. Here are a few examples:

down in the mouth—glum   put up with—tolerate
make a go of it—succeed   catch up with—overtake
give in—acquiesce   get on with it—continue

If you will *think* about your word choice, you will often find that you can improve a sentence by substituting a single-word equivalent for a colloquial phrase.

Second, we often use qualifiers to modify adjectives and adverbs. The ones most commonly used in semiformal writing are these:

GOOD STYLE: **very** irritable
quite incomprehensible
rather staid
somewhat embarrassed
fairly expensive
wholly incorrect
especially convincing
a little disturbed

Avoid the following colloquial qualifiers:

POOR STYLE: *real* intelligent   *sort of* peculiar
sure pretty   *kind of* sad
plenty excited   *awfully* conceited
awful bad   *pretty* imaginative

20C JARGON

Avoid jargon in your writing.

Jargon generally means writing that is so full of pretentious diction and abstract and technical terms that it is almost incomprehensible, even to an educated person. Here is an example of jargon from a textbook on language:

> Discussions on the possibility of a universal base (as distinct from claims about universal constraints on the form of the base component) have mainly been concerned with whether the elements specified in the rules of a universal base—if there is one—are sequential or not.

Perhaps your teacher can give you an understandable revision of this passage. This writer on language doesn't know what that writer on language meant.

In much course work (for example, in chemistry, physics, psychology, and the like) you must use technical terms because they are the only words that identify precisely what you mean. But in the rest of the sentence or paragraph use your ordinary college-level vocabulary so that your meaning is clear rather than obscure.

20D CLICHÉS

Avoid clichés in your writing.

A *cliché* is an expression that, because of long and thoughtless use, is trite, stale, worn out, and lacking in originality. For example, many people who use the phrase "feed at the public trough" don't even know that, when pigpens were common, they contained troughs to hold food for the greedy pigs, and thus many users of the phrase are unaware of its origin. Clichés are very common and have long lives because most people are too lazy or unimaginative to try to form their thoughts in their own language rather than in hackneyed phrases that are used over and over.

Here are a few examples of clichés:

ice water in his veins	a tower of strength
the acid test	the crack of dawn
the irony of fate	life is what you make it
take the bull by the horns	drunk as a lord
hard as nails	sober as a judge
a chip off the old block	a hasty retreat
straight from the shoulder	the calm before the storm
sneaking suspicion	better late than never
a crying shame	the last straw
off the beaten track	green with envy

As you write, *think* about your word choice and choose words more appropriate for your purpose than clichés.

Here are more clichés to avoid.

as fat as a pig	as meek as a lamb
as proud as a peacock	as clever (sly) as a fox
as strong as an ox	as stubborn as a mule
as slow as a snail	as courageous as a lion
as wise as an owl	as swift as an eagle

21

Exact Word Choice

21A PRECISENESS OF MEANING

Choose words that express your meaning precisely rather than approximately.

The English vocabulary is probably larger than that of any other language, and consequently it has many synonyms (words that are very similar in meaning) and very many near-synonyms. Good writers try to choose words that say precisely what they mean, whereas careless writers are content with any approximation. Some examples from student writing, with the inexact words italicized:

INEXACT: As an *uninterested* third party, Jackson *agreed* to the proposal by not voting at all.

EXACT: As a **disinterested** third party, Jackson **acquiesced** in the proposition by not voting at all.

There is some overlapping of meaning between the words in each pair, but those in the inexact version lack precision. *Uninterested* implies no interest at all, while *disinterested* suggests that he had no personal stake in the matter; he may well have been curious about the argument, however. That he did not vote requires the word *acquiesce,* which means "to remain silent"; a person who *agrees* actively gives his assent by saying yes. The last pair is almost interchangeable, and the matter may seem a minor point; *proposition,* however, generally indicates a written or formal statement as opposed to a merely spoken idea.

INEXACT: His *fond* parents *forgave* his youthful *wiles* as long as they could; finally, however, they *ceased* his *caprices.*

EXACT: His **doting** parents **condoned** his youthful **shenanigans** as long as they could; finally, however, they **put a stop to** his **mischief.**

Fond Implies loving, while *doting* suggests foolish affection brought on by old age; *forgive* equals pardon, but *condone* means overlook; *wiles* has the connotation of clever or cute, but *shenanigans* includes treachery and deceit; and action *ceases,* but people *put a stop to;* finally, *caprices* suggests impulsive or whimsical behavior, but *mischief* involves harmful conduct. The second version more clearly states what the author intended.

Do not be afraid to use new words. It is better to make mistakes and learn from them than to timidly avoid using a college-level vocabulary. Consulting a good dictionary or a thesaurus of synonyms and antonyms is a great aid in learning to choose words with the exact meanings you want.

21B   SPECIFIC AND GENERAL WORDS

Make an effort to use words as specific as your meaning calls for.

The more specific a word is, the fewer objects or concepts it applies to if it is a noun, the fewer actions or states of being it expresses if it is a verb, and the fewer qualities it signifies if it is an adjective or adverb. Of course a general word is just the opposite. For example, note how specificity increases as you pass from the very general first word to the other words in each of the following lists.

animal	talk	contented
quadruped	discuss	happy
mammal	disagree	cheerful
canine	argue	overjoyed
dog	dispute	ecstatic
mongrel	quarrel	euphoric

Animal can refer to thousands of species—millions, if insects are included—but *mongrel* refers to just one type of one species. *Talk* can apply to dozens of types of oral communication, but *quarrel* specifies a narrow range. *Contented* can apply to numerous mental states, but *euphoric* means only the ultimate in emotional happiness. General words are very important in our vocabulary; quite often a writer wants such a general word as *animal* and no other. But the more specific words you choose, the clearer your meaning and the better your style will be.

Note how the words in boldface produce a more specific statement in each of the succeeding sentences below.

> The **creature** enjoyed the **activity.**
> The **human** enjoyed the **recreation.**
> The **adult** enjoyed the **sport.**
> The **man** enjoyed **trout fishing in the stream.**
> **John** enjoyed **dry fly fishing in Catherine Creek.**

A writer may at times deliberately choose a general expression with the intent of following it up with specifics. For example, the thesis statement of an essay or paragraph is usually quite general; the paragraphs in the body of the essay or the remaining sentences in a paragraph should use specific words that give the supporting details.

21C   CONCRETE AND ABSTRACT WORDS

As much as possible, try to choose concrete words for your writing.

Technically, a concrete word is one that names an object that you can perceive with your senses, such as *book* or *kitten.* An abstract word is one that names a concept, such as *socialism* or *devotion,* or a quality apart from the object that can possess it, such as *beauty* or *gracefulness.* All concrete words can form images in the mind; that is, if you hear or read the word *horse* you have no trouble visualizing one in your mind's eye. An abstract word cannot directly form an image in your mind. For example, the word *communism* is not the name of a tangible object; it cannot form an image directly. Whatever images come into your mind when you read the word are due to the associations you have made with the word. In that sense, certain abstractions do form images in the readers' minds. For example, such words as *leer, smile, pretty, smooth, kind,* and *song* are abstractions when they are used apart from the person or thing that can wear a smile or be pretty. But they have much of the image-forming effect of such concrete words as *snake, houseboat, lake,* and *owl.* The advice for you in this section is to choose, as much as possible, concrete words or non-concrete words that have strong image-forming qualities.

Here are some examples of sentences full of abstractions, with revisions for concrete diction:

ABSTRACT: The modifications that were effected in the subject's orientation to societal mores transformed the approaches and tendencies of her existence.

CONCRETE: The changes brought about in the woman's behavior altered the color and direction of her life.

ABSTRACT: Cooper observed the large majority of all phenomena with conspicuous nonsuccess in apprehending the nature of reality.

CONCRETE: Cooper saw nearly all things as through a glass eye, darkly.

ABSTRACT: Let us render inoperable those invidious machina-
tions that endeavor to legalize the destruction of our movement.
CONCRETE: Let's defeat the legislative bills that would outlaw
our political party.

Abstractions, such as the words *modifications, mores,
apprehending,* and *invidious* in the above example sentences, need not be avoided *per se.* Individually they are
good words, and we must use abstractions like them.
However, when a sentence is little more than an accumulation of abstractions, it is usually not good writing. Concrete and image-forming diction generally improves clarity and style.

21D EUPHEMISMS

Avoid overuse of euphemisms in your writing.

A euphemism is a mild or roundabout word or expression
used instead of a more direct word or expression to make
one's language delicate and inoffensive even to a
squeamish person. Probably the most frequently used
euphemism is *passed away* for *died.* The areas that
demand euphemisms change over the decades. The
Victorians, for example, found it convenient to employ
euphemisms for bodily functions and parts of the body
that might suggest sex. Even later than 1900 a great
many genteel people would not use the words *leg* and
arm because of their sexual suggestibility and talked instead about a person's *limbs.* For one satirist, *toes*
became *twigs.* In our time we seem to need euphemisms
for the areas of social and economic standing and war.
For example, the poor nowadays are usually referred to,
at least in public documents, as the *disadvantaged* or
underprivileged; the very dull student as *educationally
handicapped;* the crazy person as *emotionally disturbed;*

old people as *senior citizens;* the sacking of a village in war as *pacification;* retreat in war as *planned withdrawal;* and lies as *inoperative statements.*

Most euphemisms probably do little harm. They may, in fact, be useful to keep from upsetting sensitive people. Most of us, no doubt, would rather hear the phrase *nasal discharge* than *snot,* or *halitosis* than *bad breath.* They can at times, however, be harmful and deceptive. As a writer and reader, you should know what they are and what they mean. Use them cautiously and never with the intent to deceive.

EUPHEMISM: Johnny tends to rely on the work of others.
MEANING: Johnny cheats.

EUPHEMISM: Ray is somewhat assertive in social situations.
MEANING: Ray is a bully.

EUPHEMISM: Oscar went to the hair stylist yesterday.
MEANING: Oscar went to the barber yesterday.

EUPHEMISM: Hitler's Germany resorted to the final solution.
MEANING: Hitler's Germany murdered 6 million humans.

21E WORDINESS

Avoid wordiness in your writing.

Write concisely as well as precisely; that is, do not ramble or use excess words. Decide clearly what you mean; then say it directly. A wordy example from student writing:

WORDY: Faulkner put the ditch in "That Evening Sun" so that when it is crossed, as it is several times, the reader can get the understanding that what is on one side of it is completely separated from what is on the other side. What is on one side is the world of the white people and what is on the other side is the world of the black people.
CONCISE: The ditch in Faulkner's "That Evening Sun," crossed several times by some of the characters, is a symbol of the immense gap between the white and black worlds.

When revising, remove unnecessarily long sentence parts. Example:

WORDY: The rock group which was brought to play in the pasture of Mr. Hollis was half-stoned by the time they got there.
CONCISE: The rock group brought to play in Mr. Hollis's pasture showed up half-stoned.

The clause beginning with *which was* is longer than the equally clear phrase *brought to play; Mr. Hollis's pasture* is less wordy than *the pasture of Mr. Hollis;* and *showed up* is much more concise than *by the time they got there.*
    Other kinds of wordiness are known as **deadwood** or **redundancy,** which means saying the same thing twice, such as *audible to the ear. To the ear* adds no meaning and is redundant because the word *audible* means "capable of being heard by the ear" (some sounds can be heard by machines but not by ears; they are not audible). Here are some examples of student sentences with deadwood or redundancy:

WORDY: I liked the biographical information *about Hardy's life* better than his *fictitious* novels.
CONCISE: I liked Hardy's biography better than his novels.

(If it is "biographical information," it is about Hardy's life"; novels are "fictitious.")

WORDY: The foreign language department has established a *new* innovation *the purpose of which is* to reduce the time we have to study written material *in the textbooks.*
CONCISE: The foreign language department has established an innovation to reduce the time we have to study written material.

("Innovative" means "new"; what is in textbooks is, naturally, written material; *the purpose of which* is simply unnecessary.)

WORDY: A metaphor is one kind of figure of speech *that is not literal* because the two *different* parts of the comparison are *completely* dissimilar *to each other.*

CONCISE: A metaphor is one kind of figure of speech because the two parts of the comparison are dissimilar.

Even the concise revisions in these examples could perhaps be written better, but their aim is to show that deadwood—needless words—can often just be omitted, with a consequent improvement in the quality of the writing.

22

Correct Word Choice

In Chapter 21 we discussed the value of choosing words for the exact meaning you want, rather than words that only approximately express your meaning. In this chapter we will deal with the choice of wrong words—words that, if taken literally, do not even approximately express your meaning. For example, if you ask someone for change for a dollar and receive nineteen nickels, your request will have been approximately met; but if instead you receive a handful of pebbles, your dollar's change is not even approximately right but wholly incorrect.

22A MALAPROPISMS

Consult a dictionary, if necessary, to prevent use of malapropisms.

A malapropism, named after a character in an eighteenth-century play who mangled the language in almost every speech, is simply a word wholly incorrect for the meaning intended but that usually has some sort of humorous application, such as some similarity in sound. A couple of examples are *a shrewd awakening* for *a rude awakening* and *you lead and we'll precede* for *you lead and we'll proceed (behind you).*

Here are some examples of student malapropisms, with the malapropisms italicized:

MALAPROPISM: The fans were now supporting our team *voraciously.*
RIGHT: The fans were now supporting our team **vociferously.**

MALAPROPISM: He was driving under the *affluence* of alcohol.
RIGHT: He was driving under the **influence** of alcohol.

MALAPROPISM: Harold's *alligator* shoes gave him added height.
RIGHT: Harold's **elevator** shoes gave him added height.

MALAPROPISM: *Designating* the flag is now a Federal offense.
RIGHT: **Desecrating** the flag is now a Federal offense.

MALAPROPISM: I have been absent for the last week because I am going to get married and have been to San Francisco to get my *torso* ready.
RIGHT: I have been absent for the last week because I am going to get married and have been to San Francisco to get my **trousseau** ready.

Such boners are fairly common because people often misinterpret the sounds they hear and give no thought to the real meanings of the words they misuse. The most common malapropism, perhaps, is *take it for granite* instead of *take it for granted.* But perhaps the funniest of all is the Sunday school child's singing about *the cross-eyed bear* when the hymn "Gladly the Cross I'd Bear" was sung. The dictionary cannot help you avoid such malapropisms as those, but it can keep you from confusing such words as, say, *tortuous* and *torturous.* Comedians often use malapropisms in their routines. In serious writing they interfere with clear meaning. Value your dictionary and use it.

22B   CONFUSED WORDS

Do not confuse a word with one similar to it in sound or meaning or spelling.

A number of pairs or trios of words are frequently confused and cannot be labeled malapropisms (which are seldom repeated). Check both the list in Section 16G (for spelling purposes) and this list to avoid producing incorrect rather than merely inappropriate word choice.

accept is a verb meaning "to receive."
except is a preposition meaning "not included."

all ready is an indefinite pronoun plus adjective meaning "everyone or everything is prepared."
already is an adverb meaning "at or before this time."

all together is an indefinite pronoun plus adjective meaning "everyone in unison."
altogether is an adverb meaning "completely."

allude is a verb meaning "to mention indirectly." *Allusion* is the noun.
refer is a verb meaning "to mention directly." *Reference* is the noun.

anyway is an adverb meaning "in any case."
any way is a noun phrase meaning "whatever way possible."

beside is a preposition meaning "at the side of."
besides is a preposition or adverb meaning "in addition to."

broadcast is a verb with the principal parts *broadcast, broadcast, broadcast. Broadcasted* is nonstandard.

burst is a verb with the principal parts *burst, burst, burst. Bust* and *busted* are nonstandard for *burst.* (*Busted* is also a slang word for arrested.)

cite is a verb meaning "to mention or refer to."
site is a noun meaning "a place."

colloquialism is a noun meaning "a word or phrase suitable for informal use."
localism is a noun meaning "a word or expression used only in one locality or region."

complement is a noun (and verb) meaning "something that completes or makes a whole."
compliment is a noun (and verb) meaning "praise given."

conscience is a noun meaning "a sense of right and wrong."
conscious is an adjective meaning "awake or alert."

could of, would of are nonstandard spellings of "could've (have)" and "would've (have)."

council is a noun meaning "an official, deliberative group."
counsel is a verb (and noun) meaning "to give advice." *Counselor* comes from *counsel.*

credible is an adjective meaning "believable."
creditable is an adjective meaning "worthy of praise."
credulous is an adjective meaning "willing to believe readily or easily imposed upon."

delusion is a noun meaning "a false belief."
illusion is a noun meaning "a deceptive appearance or false impression."

discreet means "careful about what one does or says"
discrete means "separate and distinct" or "one by one"

disinterested is an adjective meaning "impartial or having no personal interest."
uninterested is an adjective meaning "not interested."

farther is an adverb pertaining to physical distance.
further is an adverb pertaining to degree of advancement in ideas, concepts, and so on.

forecast is a verb with the principal parts *forecast, forecast, forecast. Forecasted* is nonstandard.

hanged is the past tense and past participle of the verb *hang* when it means execution.
hung is the past tense and past participle of the verb *hang* for all other meanings.

imply is a verb meaning "to suggest or hint."
infer is a verb meaning "to draw a conclusion or inference about."

inside of is colloquial for *within.*

irregardless is nonstandard. Use *regardless.*

kind of, sort of are colloquial phrases for *rather* or *somewhat.*

later is an adverb or adjective meaning "at a time after a specified time."
latter is an adjective (and noun) meaning "nearest the end or the last mentioned."

liable is an adjective meaning "responsible or legally bound or likely to occur."
libel is a verb meaning "to slander in print" and a noun meaning "slanderous articles."

lie, lay See Section 8C.

loose is an adjective meaning "not tight."
lose is a verb meaning "to mislay or be deprived of."

marital is an adjective meaning "pertaining to marriage."
martial is an adjective meaning "pertaining to military operations."

maybe is an adverb meaning "perhaps or possibly."
may be is a verb form indicating possibility.

moral is an adjective meaning "right or ethical."
morale is a noun meaning "a mental attitude or condition."

nohow is nonstandard for *anyway.*

oral means "spoken." It is preferable in that sense to *verbal,* which refers to both oral and written language.

passed is the past tense and past participle of the verb *to pass.*
past is a noun meaning "of a former time" and a preposition meaning "passing beside."

persecute is a verb meaning "to harass cruelly or annoy persistently."
prosecute is a verb meaning "to bring suit against."

principal is an adjective meaning "chief or most important" and a noun meaning "head of a school" or "money used as capital."
principle is a noun meaning "a rule or doctrine."

quiet is an adjective meaning "not noisy."
quite is a qualifier meaning "entirely or almost entirely."

sensual is an adjective meaning "lewd or carnal."
sensuous is an adjective meaning "characterized by sense impressions."

set, sit See Section 8C.

than is a subordinating conjunction used in a comparison.
then is an adverb of time or a conjunctive adverb meaning "therefore."

For words not on this list, consult your dictionary. Form the habit of relying on your dictionary and not just guessing.

22C INCORRECT IDIOMS

Avoid incorrect idioms in your writing.

Strictly defined, an idiom is a construction "peculiar" to a language, not understandable from the meanings of the individual words in it, and not literally translatable into another language. For example, in the expressions *I ran across an old friend,* neither the verb nor the preposition has its regular meaning. Instead, *ran across* means "to encounter by chance" and is an English idiom.

Again, *He put up his visiting relatives in the guest room* would produce a hilarious construction if translated literally into another language.

Idiomatic English is English phrasing that is natural, normal, and clearly understandable to a native speaker of English. We normally think of English idioms as containing at least one preposition, or a word that looks like a preposition, and that is the way we will consider idioms in this chapter on correct word choice. Thus, if (as once happened) a student should write *this contradicts with my opinion,* we would say the idiom was faulty, for native speakers would write *this contradicts my opinion.*

Faulty idioms are far more common in writing than in conversation, possibly because the writers are striving hard to express their thoughts in writing and make errors *because* they are striving so hard. Here are some faulty idioms from student papers.

FAULTY IDIOM: Poe has been acclaimed by many *of being* a
   great writer.
RIGHT: Poe has been acclaimed by many **to be** a great writer.

FAULTY IDIOM: Poe is *attributed to being* the originator of the
   detective story.
RIGHT: Poe is **considered** the originator of the detective story.

FAULTY IDIOM: Military service should not be *likened with* a
   prison sentence.
RIGHT: Military service should not be **likened to** a prison sentence.

FAULTY IDIOM: Thoreau would have died for the ideals *for which he was so radically supporting.*

RIGHT: Thoreau would have died for the ideals **which he so radically supported.**

No rules can be given to keep you from writing a faulty idiom occasionally. The best advice is to listen carefully to those whose speech habits you admire, to think calmly and without panic as you write, and to proofread your work carefully.

22D OMITTED WORDS

Do not carelessly omit a needed word.

Examples:

OMITTED WORD: The man bought the car from me was too naive to check it thoroughly.

RIGHT: The man **who** bought the car from me was too naive to check it thoroughly.

OMITTED WORD: Jane was happy about the outcome but my parents bitter about it.

RIGHT: Jane was happy about the outcome but my parents **were** bitter about it.

In the correct sentences the boldface words are needed.

SECTION FIVE

EFFECTIVE SENTENCES

23

Faulty Sentence Structure

Good writing is a complex mixture of many components, but at its heart is the sentence. The great English states-man and writer Sir Winston Churchill called the English sentence "a noble thing," and it is a truism that anyone who can write really good sentences can write longer pas-sages well too. Sentences, however, are so complex that many things can go wrong with them. But students can learn to write sentences without faulty structure, and thus we have this chapter on the main kinds of errors in sen-tence structure.

23A MIXED SENTENCE STRUCTURE

Do not inconsistently shift structure in the middle of a sentence.

Mixed sentence structure usually occurs when a writer begins a sentence with one kind of structure, forgets that structure somewhere along the way, and completes the sentence with a different, incompatible kind of structure. Here is an example from a student paper:

MIXED STRUCTURE: Financial aid has made it possible for me to continue my education and not finding a job right away.

The shift in structure comes after the conjunction *and,* which indicates that either a second independent clause will follow or a structure beginning with *to.* A unified structure might have been maintained in either of these two ways:

RIGHT: Financial aid has made it possible for me to continue my education, and **I did not have to find a job right away.** (a compound sentence with two independent clauses)

RIGHT: Financial aid has made it possible for me to continue my education and **to postpone finding a job right away.** (a simple sentence with two infinitive phrases in the predicate)

Here are other examples from student writing of mixed sentence structure, with revisions:

MIXED STRUCTURE: A golfer who is capable of shooting par and avoiding the rough gives him a sense of accomplishment toward the game.

RIGHT: A golfer who is capable of shooting par and avoiding the rough **develops a sense of accomplishment in regard to the game.**

Long and involved subjects sometimes lead to confusion. The writer apparently lost track of the single subject *golfer* and thought that *shooting par and avoiding the rough* required the verb *gives.* The revision provides a suitable predicate.

MIXED STRUCTURE: All of these facts boil down to that science is playing a major role in our lives.

RIGHT: All of these facts mean that science is playing a major role in our lives.

In the mixed sentence the student writer failed to compose a subject and verb combination that would take the noun clause *that . . . lives* as a direct object. The revision provides a suitable subject and verb.

MIXED STRUCTURE: Those writers that Poe predicted would never make it, we have never even heard their names in our time.

RIGHT: Those writers that Poe predicted would never make it have never been heard of in our time.

In the mixed sentence the student writer composed the long but satisfactory subject *Those . . . it* and then, instead of providing a predicate for the subject, inconsistently continued with a complete independent clause. The revision changes the independent clause into a predicate that fits the subject.

23B FAULTY PREDICATION

Be sure that your subject and predicate are compatible.

The grammatical term *predication* means the fitting of a predicate to a subject to make an independent clause (or sentence), such as this grammatically correct sentence:

The mayor of our town / is also the chief of police

The slash (/) separates the subject from the predicate.

When a subject and predicate are not compatible, the error known as faulty predication occurs. For example,

Courageously / is a time of happiness

is obviously a nonsentence because its predication is faulty; the adverb *courageously* cannot serve as the subject of the predicate *is a time of happiness*—or, for that matter, as the subject of any predicate. Equally a nonsentence is this student's creation:

FAULTY PREDICATION: Through God's creation alone / is the only concept of God that man has.

The prepositional phrase *through God's creation alone* will not function as the subject of the predicate that follows. The student may have meant to say something like this:

RIGHT: The only concept of God that man can have / lies in God's creation of the universe.

However, as is often the case in sentences with faulty predication, what the writer meant to say is not entirely clear.

Here are some other examples from student writing of faulty predication, with revisions:

FAULTY PREDICATION: Composition and impact were awarded first prize for the picture.

The composition and impact did not win first prize; the picture did. The subjects do not fit the predicate. The sentence should read something like this:

RIGHT: The picture / was awarded first prize because of its composition and impact.

Another example:

FAULTY PREDICATION: My reaction to being in a large English class / seemed a little strange and different.

The predication is faulty because it was the class and not the student's reaction that seemed strange and different. A better version:

RIGHT: Being in such a large English class / was a strange and different experience for me.

Additional examples:

FAULTY PREDICATION: Another misconception / is when we try to visualize God.

FAULTY PREDICATION: Characterization / is where I think Faulkner succeeded best.

FAULTY PREDICATION: Because my alarm clock didn't go off is why I was late for work.

FAULTY PREDICATION: The reason he drove through the intersection is because the stop sign was hidden by a tree.

These are examples of the faulty *is when, is where, is why, is because* kinds of sentences. Avoid these expressions. They reflect poor style as well as faulty predication. Usually a noun or noun substitute or an adjective must follow the verb *is*. Sometimes such sentences must be recast completely to provide proper predication.

RIGHT: Another misconception / is that human beings can actually visualize God.

RIGHT: Characterization / is the best aspect of Faulkner's fiction.

RIGHT: I / was late for work because my alarm clock didn't go off.

RIGHT: He / drove through the intersection because a tree hid the stop sign.

23C   FAULTY PARALLELISM

Make sure that the constituents in any series in your sentences are parallel in structure.

In sentence structure, parallelism means the use of two or more similar constituents in a series, usually with a coordinating connective between the last two constituents. For example:

RIGHT: **Having no money** but **wanting to attend the festival,** I considered selling my typewriter.

The two boldface constituents are parallel in structure; they are similar in form (both begin with *-ing* words) and in function (both modify the subject of the main clause).

When two or more *dissimilar* constituents are in a series, faulty parallelism results. An example from student writing, with the constituents in faulty parallelism italicized:

FAULTY PARALLELISM: *If a man is brilliant in a specific field* but *having no general knowledge,* he may be quite useless.

Here a dependent clause and a phrase are joined by *but,* with faulty parallelism the result. The sentence should read like this:

RIGHT: If a man **is brilliant in a specific field** but **does not have general knowledge,** he may be useless.

Now two predicates (with the subject *man*) are in correct parallelism.

Other examples from student work:

FAULTY PARALLELISM: When we entertain *friends, parents,* and *behave ourselves,* we are praised.

RIGHT: When we **entertain friends and parents** and **behave ourselves,** we are praised.

The incorrect sentence has two nouns and one predicate in faulty parallelism. Two proper sets of parallel constituents are in the correct sentence: the boldface predicates and the two nouns *friends* and *parents* in the first predicate.

FAULTY PARALLELISM: Local color was flourishing, *with Harte writing about California* and *Cable wrote about Louisiana.*

RIGHT: Local color was flourishing, with **Harte writing about California** and **Cable writing about Louisiana.**

The incorrect sentence has a prepositional phrase and an independent clause in faulty parallelism. The correct sentence has two objects of the preposition *with* in proper parallel structure.

23D   DANGLING MODIFIERS

Do not let an introductory or terminal constituent dangle with no word or word group to modify.

Usually when a sentence opens with an introductory constituent that is not the subject, the constituent modifies the subject that follows. Example:

RIGHT: Having seen the menu, I gave my order immediately.

In such structures the subject of the main clause does whatever is mentioned in the introductory expression. Who saw the menu? I did. The sentence meaning is clear. But suppose the sentence were written like this:

DANGLING MODIFIER: *Having seen the menu,* my order was given immediately.

Now the sentence says that my order saw the menu—obviously untrue. The introductory expression dangles; it has no word to modify.

Here is another example of a dangling modifier, with the dangler italicized. Note how the dangling modifier in the first sentence falsely says that the children (*they*) brought up the children, but the revised sentence correctly identifies who brings up the children.

DANGLING MODIFIER: *By bringing children up together in schools of equal opportunity,* they will become friendly.

RIGHT: By bringing children up together in schools of equal opportunity, we allow them to become friendly.

To repeat: avoid dangling modifiers by making sure the subject of the main clause clearly refers to the action or condition mentioned in the introductory expression. In the following example, *shut-ins and patients* do not provide security; rather, *personal-advice columns* do.

DANGLING MODIFIER: *Besides providing security for active people,* shut-ins and hospital patients get pleasure from personal-advice columns.

RIGHT: Besides providing security for active people, personal-advice columns give pleasure to shut-ins and hospital patients.

You may correct an otherwise dangling modifier by providing it with its own subject and a finite verb (one that shows tense or time of action), thus changing it into a clause.

DANGLING MODIFIER: The church is a good place to go, *when unsettled in mind.*

The sentence seems to say that the church is unsettled in mind, and thus the terminal constituent dangles. Here is a revision:

RIGHT: The church is a good place to go when you are unsettled in mind.

In this revision the dangler has been altered in structure so that it no longer dangles but delivers clear meaning.

23E   MISPLACED MODIFIERS

Always place a modifier in a sentence so that the word or word group it modifies is immediately clear.

Most sentences in good writing have a number of modifiers, and most modifiers come as close to the word they modify as possible. The good writer must give thought to the placement of modifiers if the meaning is to be immediately clear. For example, consider this sentence from a news report:

MISPLACED MODIFIER: Collins was told that his services would no longer be needed *by the personnel officer.*

When the sentence is considered in isolation, it seems clear that the personnel officer will no longer need Collins's services (though others in the company may). But the whole report made it clear that the personnel officer was firing Collins. Thus the writer misplaced the modifier *by the personnel officer* and no doubt momentarily confused thousands of readers. The italicized phrase should have been placed after *told.*

Here are some other examples of misplaced modifiers, with the modifiers italicized:

MISPLACED MODIFIER: Your interesting letter regarding the honors program *of December 2* reached me today.

Of December 2 should come directly after *letter,* for the writer was specifying the date of the letter, not of the honors program.

MISPLACED MODIFIER: They can easily destroy this magnificent creation, which represents 3000 years of careful work *with the press of a button.*

The work was not done with the press of a button. For immediate clarity, the italicized phrase should come after *destroy* or at the very beginning of the sentence.

MISPLACED MODIFIER: I feel that I am going to succeed in all my future goals *today.*

For instant clarity, *today* should come directly after *feel* or at the beginning of the sentence.

MISPLACED MODIFIER: Dickinson says that earth's heaven is nature *in her work.*

The sentence makes no sense unless the italicized phrase is placed after *says* or at the beginning of the sentence.

MISPLACED MODIFIER: *After conducting a long search,* a used car was bought by my daughter *whose body was in good shape.*

This sentence contains both a dangling modifier and a misplaced modifier. The used car did not conduct a long search, and thus the introductory expression dangles. It may or may not be true that my daughter's body is in good shape (as the misplaced modifier suggests), but the intended meaning appears in the correct sentence that follows.

RIGHT: After conducting a long search, my daughter bought a used car whose body was in good shape.

A final example:

UNCLEAR MODIFIER: We told Fred and Harriet *on Wednesday* we would leave.
CLEAR: On Wednesday we told Fred and Harriet we would leave.
CLEAR: We told Fred and Harriet we would leave on Wednesday.

24

Pronoun Reference

A pronoun gets its meaning through reference to some other word or word group, which is known as the pronoun's **antecedent.** Since the pronoun does not have meaning of its own, its reference—or antecedent—must be unmistakably clear if the sentence is to deliver clear meaning. Furthermore, even when its meaning is clear, a pronoun must be properly used if the sentence is to be effective and stylistically acceptable. Sentence effectiveness is easily diminished by faulty pronoun reference.

24A REFERENCE TO TITLES

Do not use a pronoun in the opening sentence of a paper to refer to the title or a noun in the title.

Though themes, essays, and term papers should have suitable titles, such titles are not part of the composition itself; they are added only *after* the body of the paper has been written. Almost always a paper should be opened as though the title were not stated. Here, from a student's work, is an illustration of how *not* to use pronoun reference to a title:

TOPIC: Write an essay about one of your favorite pastimes.
TITLE: Creating Designs on Ceramics
IMPROPER REFERENCE IN OPENING SENTENCE: When you learn the technique of applying design material to *them,* you are ready to work on your artistry.

The *them* in the opening sentence, referring to *ceramics* (or does it refer to *designs?*) in the title, produces a particularly ineffective sentence and theme introduction.

Sometimes a careless student will even choose a topic from several written on a blackboard or handout sheet, not compose a title at all, and then begin the paper with a reference to the topic, while the teacher does not know which topic has been picked. For example, after being handed a list of seven topics to choose from, one student once opened a titleless paper with this sentence:

IMPROPER REFERENCE IN OPENING SENTENCE: First, I think *it* should be discussed more before *they* make a decision.

The *it* and *they* in the opening sentence ruined the theme at the outset.

24B AMBIGUOUS REFERENCE

Do not use a pronoun so that it can meaningfully refer to either of two nouns or word groups.

Ambiguity means having two possible meanings, and pronoun reference is ambiguous when there is more than one clearly possible antecedent for the pronoun. Example from a student paper:

AMBIGUOUS REFERENCE: When she met Mrs. Barry in the coffee shop, *she* immediately asked why *she* had failed the Writing Proficiency Examination.

Do the *she*'s refer to the professor or the student? Later sentences made the reference clear, but it was at first ambiguous and thus destroyed sentence effectiveness. A revision:

CLEAR REFERENCE: When she met Mrs. Barry in the coffee shop, **Beth** immediately asked why she had failed the Writing Proficiency Examination.

The second *she* is now unmistakably clear in its reference.

Sometimes ambiguous reference occurs when a pronoun is only understood and not stated. Example from an advertisement, with the understood pronoun in brackets:

AMBIGUOUS REFERENCE: The trunk on a Dart is actually bigger than the one on many full-sized cars. And a family of five fits inside [it] nicely.

The ad writer intended the understood *it* to refer to *Dart* but it seems to refer to *trunk.* The writer should have put *the car* after *inside.* Also note the inconsistency of specifying *one* trunk for *many* full-sized cars.

24C FAULTY BROAD REFERENCE

Avoid using *this, that, which,* and *it* with vague, indefinite, or ambiguous reference.

Broad reference means that a pronoun does not refer to an individual noun but to a whole idea expressed in an independent clause or word group. Broad reference is completely acceptable when it is clear, and, indeed, it is very common. Examples:

CLEAR BROAD REFERENCE: *The Old Man and the Sea* depicts man in single combat with nature, **which** is a common theme in Hemingway's fiction.

CLEAR BROAD REFERENCE: The issue was one of morality, not legality. **This** became evident in the debate.

CLEAR BROAD REFERENCE: Had I worked harder, **it** still would not have helped.

The *which, this,* and *it* clearly refer to whole ideas, not individual nouns, and the broad reference is acceptable, or even desirable.

Often, however, broad reference is vague, indefinite, or ambiguous, and then it destroys sentence effectiveness. First, here is an example from a nationally circulated advertisement:

FAULTY BROAD REFERENCE: Any food you buy that you do not like or use reduces the amount of your savings, *which* after all is the main purpose of our plan.

The *which* seems to refer to the idea of *reducing the amount of your savings,* whereas obviously the writer had in mind *increasing the amount of your savings.* The common remark "You know what I mean" is no excuse for such bad writing.

Here, taken from a magazine, is an example of faulty broad reference of *it:*

FAULTY BROAD REFERENCE: The odds are that such youngsters will drop out of school eight or ten years later with little to show for *it* but the experience of failure.

The *it* cannot logically refer to the idea of *dropping out of school.* Perhaps the writer meant to say "with little to show for their time but the experience of failure."

The pronoun *this* seems to be most misused in broad reference in student writing. Example:

FAULTY BROAD REFERENCE: Take for example the TV ad wherein they shave off the sand from a piece of sandpaper. How do we know whether *that* is true? Many people, however, never give *this* a second thought.

The *that* is much too vague in its reference, and the *this* is hopelessly indefinite. A revision:

CLEAR MEANING: Take for example the TV ad in which sand is shaved off a piece of sandpaper. How do we know the shaving is not faked? Many people, however, never give a second thought to the truthfulness of TV ads.

Another example:

FAULTY BROAD REFERENCE: I will not try to convince you that all television programs are worthwhile. *This* is a fallacy.

The writer probably means: "That all television programs are worthwhile is a fallacy," but the faulty use of *this* destroys the effectiveness of the passage.

One more example:

FAULTY BROAD REFERENCE: When someone mentions voter apathy, most people think of minority groups. *This* is not true.

The *this* is so indefinitely used that the reader must supply a sentence or two of his own to see that the writer means that voter apathy is not limited to minority groups.

So, take great care with your use of the broad reference *this* and also with the broad references, *that, which,* and *it.*

24D REMOTE REFERENCE

Avoid using a pronoun so far removed from its antecedent that the reader has to pause to determine its meaning.

Example from student writing:

REMOTE REFERENCE: On the first mild day of spring we decided to go boating on the lake. We found that some vandals had damaged our boathouse and some gear, but we were able to make quick repairs and thus were not disappointed in our first sail on *it* for the year.

The *it* is so far removed from its antecedent, *lake* (or does it refer to an unstated *sailboat*?), that the reader momentarily stumbles and must reread to be sure of the meaning.

And here is an example from a cookbook:

REMOTE REFERENCE: To enhance the flavor of roast chicken, spill a glass of white wine and sprinkle parsley over *it* while roasting.

Aside from the fact that the sentence seems to imply that the wine may be spilled on the floor and that the cook is roasting, the *it* is too far removed from its antecedent, *roast chicken,* for clear reference.

24E IMPLIED ANTECEDENTS

Do not use a pronoun with an implied antecedent.

Pronouns may refer to whole ideas but, in good writing at least, they should not refer to adjectives or to antecedents implied and not stated. Example:

IMPLIED ANTECEDENT: Professor Stansbury is humorous and *it* makes her classes popular.

Though the meaning of the sentence is not obscured, *it* refers to the adjective *humorous,* a stylistically undesirable technique in English. The reader is forced to supply the noun *humor* for *it* to have an antecedent. A revision:

BETTER STYLE: The humor Professor Stansbury displays in her classes makes them popular.

Another example:

IMPLIED ANTECEDENT: I liked Hawaii partly because *they* were all so friendly.

The absence of *Hawaiians* as an antecedent for *they* creates a poor sentence.
Two examples:

IMPLIED ANTECEDENT: "The Second Choice" was about a young girl who fell in love and then lost *him.*
IMPLIED ANTECEDENT: In "The Grass So Little Has to Do" Dickinson seems to envy the simplicity of nature and expresses *it* in the last line of the poem.

In the first sentence, *him* is meant to refer to *lover,* who is not mentioned. The *it* in the second sentence has no noun to refer to. Presumably the writer intended it to mean "envy," but the *envy* used in the sentence is a verb. A pronoun cannot refer to a verb. The sentence can be corrected by substituting "that envy" for *it*.

24F *WHAT* AS A PRONOUN

Do not use *what* as a substitute for the pronouns *who* and *that*.

Example:

WRONG: The guy *what* sold me that car was a crook.
RIGHT: The guy **who** sold me that car was a crook.

25

Faulty Comparisons

Comparisons, which must consist of at least two constituents even if one is understood, occur frequently in our
language, and three kinds of errors are commonly made
in their use. (See Section 5D for pronoun forms used in
comparative constructions.) These errors diminish sentence effectiveness considerably.

25A INCOMPLETE COMPARISONS

**Avoid incomplete comparisons that in effect make
nonsensical sentences.**

Aside from the conjunctions *than, as,* and *like* and the
prepositions *like* and *from* used to form comparisons, two
other words—*other* and *else*—frequently help form comparisons. These comparative words should not be omitted.

Advertising copy often omits the *than* part of a comparison, perhaps intentionally. Example:

INCOMPLETE COMPARISON: El Ropos smoke more smoothly.

The ad writer wants the reader to understand *than other cigars,* but such incomplete comparisons should be avoided in college writing. For example, don't write such a sentence as

INCOMPLETE COMPARISON: Attending a private college is different.

without specifying what it is different from. Finish the comparison.

COMPLETE COMPARISON: Attending a private college is different from going to a state university.

A second kind of incomplete comparison is perhaps even less acceptable because it forms a nonsensical (even though understandable) sentence. This is the kind of comparison that says that one thing is longer or kinder or more extensive than itself. Example from student writing:

INCOMPLETE COMPARISON: Nixon traveled to more foreign countries than any president.

Since Nixon was a president, the term *any president* also includes him. The sentence literally says that Nixon traveled to more foreign countries than even Nixon did. If we apply rigorous logic, this is nonsense. The sentence is more effective if written with *other,* a comparison-completing word.

COMPLETE COMPARISON: Nixon traveled to more foreign countries than any **other** president.

Another example:

INCOMPLETE COMPARISON: My father has captured more mountain lions than anybody in our county.

The student's father presumably lives in "our county." Thus the sentence says her father has captured more mountain lions than even her father, which is logical non-sense. The comparison-completing word *else* makes the sentence much more effective:

COMPLETE COMPARISON: My father has captured more moun-tain lions than anybody **else** in our county.

Now the comparison is complete and the sentence much improved.

Remember not to omit the words *other* and *else* in comparisons that call for one or the other of them.

25B FALSE COMPARISONS

Do not compose sentences that express false com-parisons.

A comparison says that one thing is similar to, greater or lesser than, or different from another. But when the two parts of the comparison are incompatible for comparative purposes, a false comparison occurs and produces a bad sentence. Example:

FALSE COMPARISON: The old trapper had a face like a bulldog, its jowls hanging loosely.

Though a reader may know what was intended, this sen-tence literally compares a face and an animal. Using the possessive (which implies the missing word) corrects the sentence so that a face is compared to a face.

TRUE COMPARISON: The old trapper had a face like a bulldog's, its jowls hanging loosely.

Here are some other examples:

FALSE COMPARISON: We were searching for paintings more like Van Gogh.
FALSE COMPARISON: My uncle farms like the nineteenth cen-tury.
FALSE COMPARISON: Today's students' behavior is just like their parents.

Was Van Gogh a painting? Did the nineteenth century farm? Is behavior a parent? No. Sometimes using another form of the possessive, or supplying a clear subject and predicate for the second item, or rewriting the sentence completely will produce a true comparison as well as good style.

TRUE COMPARISON: We were searching for paintings more like **those of** Van Gogh.

TRUE COMPARISON: My uncle farms much as **people did** in the nineteenth century.

TRUE COMPARISON: Students today behave just as their parents did a generation ago.

25C OMITTED COMPARATIVE WORDS

In a double comparison, do not omit a needed comparative word, such as *than* or *as*.

Sometimes a double comparison calls for two different comparative words, and careless writers often omit one of the two. Example from a student paper:

OMITTED COMPARATIVE WORD: This generic brand is as good if not better than the brand we used to buy.

COMPLETE DOUBLE COMPARISON: This generic brand is as good **as** if not better than the brand we used to buy.

Both parts of the *as . . . as* construction must be present to complete the comparison.

Mentally removing *if not better than* from the sentence shows that both parts of the *as . . . as* construction must be present. Use the same test in the following examples (that is, remove *or at least as difficult as*) to note that *than* must be used to complete the comparison.

OMITTED COMPARATIVE WORD: My piano class this quarter is more difficult, or at least as difficult as, my philosophy class.

COMPLETE DOUBLE COMPARISON: My piano class this quarter is more difficult **than,** or at least as difficult as, my philosophy class.

26

Mature
and Well-Formed
Sentences

Avoiding errors and weaknesses in writing is important, but such successful avoidance does not guarantee good writing. Various positive qualities in a writer's sentences are also needed if the writing is to be of good quality. Our point here can be made clearer by drawing a comparison with marriage. In marriage, it is desirable for the partners to avoid quarrels, fights, and other conflicts. But does such avoidance guarantee a happy marriage? No. In addition to avoiding, as much as possible, various conflicts, the partners need to show affection for each other, to love, to share, to be delighted, at least part of the time, with each other's company. The positive and the negative: both are important in many aspects of human behavior. In this chapter we will discuss the sentence from various positive points of view.

26A   SENTENCE EXPANSIONS

Strive to achieve maturity of sentence structure; avoid excessive use of short, simple sentences.

Though short, simple sentences have their place in good writing and are often needed for the writer to achieve a desired effect, most sentences in good writing are composed of more than one simple independent clause. Various kinds of sentence expansions (large sentence constituents) allow us to express two or more full ideas in one well-composed sentence.

Little children speak or write mostly in run-on simple sentences strung together by *and.* For example, a child might tell a story in this fashion:

> Grandpa came and he took me to the zoo and we watched the elephants and I held out a peanut and one elephant stuck out his nose and he took it and he ate it and he dropped the shell on the ground.

But a person who has matured in his language usage would try to *compose* a sentence with various sentence expansions attached to one or two independent clauses. Example:

> When Grandpa came, he took me to the zoo where we watched the elephants. When I offered a peanut, one of them stuck out his trunk, took it, and ate it, dropping the shell on the ground.

The foregoing is an extremely simple illustration, but it expresses an important point. As a writer, you will want to give attention to composing mature sentences with various kinds of sentence expansions or large constituents. You need not know the names of such constituents in order to *use* them well, but we need to label such expansions in order to talk about them. Section 26A offers a variety of methods to help you develop mature prose.

26A1   Compound Structures

In addition to joining two independent clauses into a compound sentence (see Section 1B3), remember that you can also compound smaller parts of sentences: single words, subjects, predicates, whole phrases, and even dependent clauses. Examples:

SIMPLE SENTENCES: The fish inspected the bait. The fish decided not to take it.

COMPOUND SENTENCE: **The fish inspected the bait,** but **he decided not to take it.**

COMPOUND PREDICATE: **The fish inspected the bait** but **decided not to take it.** (No new subject)

COMPOUND SUBJECT: **The fish** and **the fisherman** were both experienced.

COMPOUND PHRASES: The fisherman cast his lure **to the right** and **to the left.**

COMPOUND OBJECT: That day he caught only **an old boot** and **a piece of driftwood.**

You perhaps miss more opportunities than you realize to tighten your style through use of more compound structures.

26A2   Appositives

An appositive is essentially a noun-repeater, in that it defines or explains a noun that it is said to be in apposition to. Example:

SIMPLE SENTENCES: My car still gets thirty miles to the gallon on the highway. It is an old Volkswagen.

APPOSITIVE: My car, **an old Volkswagen,** still gets thirty miles to the gallon on the highway.

Chances are that you will be able to improve the quality of your writing considerably by using appositives more frequently.

26A3   Adjective Clauses

An adjective clause is introduced by one of the relative pronouns (*who, whom, whose, which,* and *that*), which usually has a noun antecedent in another part of the full sentence. Since it contains a subject and predicate, the adjective clause expresses a full idea, but one that is subordinated to an independent clause or a part of the main sentence. Like all the constituents we are illustrating in Section 26A, the adjective clause allows us to *expand* a simple sentence and thus achieve more mature sentence structure. Example:

SIMPLE SENTENCES: The lab assistant brought out the equipment. We were to use it in the day's experiment.
ADJECTIVE CLAUSE: The lab assistant brought out the equipment **that we were to use in the day's experiment.**

The superiority of the structure of the second version is plain.

26A4   Adjective Phrases

An adjective phrase is composed of an adjective functioning as a headword, with modifiers clustering around it. Since it is a phrase, it does not have a subject and a predicate. As a sentence expansion, however, it expresses a full idea. Example:

SIMPLE SENTENCES: Art Hempel was tall for his age. He played varsity basketball in his freshman year.
ADJECTIVE PHRASE: Art Hempel, **tall for his age,** played varsity basketball in his freshman year.

The adjective phrase draws its meaning from *Art Hempel was* and thus expresses a full idea.

26A5   Adverb Clauses

An adverb clause is introduced by one of the subordinating conjunctions—*because, since, unless, if, though,* and many others. These subordinating conjunctions express such relationships as cause-and-result, contrast, condition, and time between the idea in the adverb clause and the independent clause or a part of the main sentence. Example:

SIMPLE SENTENCES: I was waiting for Howard to bring the boat around. I caught three fish from the dock.

ADVERB CLAUSE: **While I was waiting for Howard to bring the boat around,** I caught three fish from the dock.

Since the adverb clause has a subject and a predicate, it contains a full idea. The subordinating conjunction *while* expresses the proper relationship between the ideas.

26A6 Noun Clauses

Noun clauses usually do not function as sentence expansions but as subjects or direct objects in independent clauses. However, as appositives they can, and often do, function as expansions. Example:

SIMPLE SENTENCES: The Yazidis' basic belief is that the world is at this time controlled by the devil. This belief derives from their observation of the horrendous state of the world.

NOUN CLAUSE: The basic belief of the Yazidis—**that the world is at this time controlled by the devil**—derives from their observation of the horrendous state of the world.

The use of the noun clause as an appositive produces superior sentence structure. In the first of the simple sentences, the noun clause *that the world is at this time controlled by the devil* functions as a predicate noun and is thus not a sentence expansion.

26A7 Prepositional Phrases

Often a prepositional phrase with a complex structure functions as a sentence modifier. As such it expresses a full idea and is a sentence expansion. Example:

SIMPLE SENTENCES: Robertson had phenomenal skill in playing the trombone. He was also our orchestra conductor.

PREPOSITIONAL PHRASE: **In addition to his phenomenal skill in playing the trombone,** Robertson was also our orchestra conductor.

Note that the relationship between the ideas in the simple sentences is not expressed, whereas the sentence with the prepositional phrase does express that relationship.

26A8 Verbal Phrases

Various kinds of verbal phrases (the technical names of which you don't need to know) serve as sentence expansions. Examples:

SIMPLE SENTENCES: We had accomplished our objectives in a single meeting. We cancelled the second meeting.

VERBAL PHRASE: **Having accomplished our objectives in a single meeting,** we cancelled the second.

Two points are to be noted here. First, the verbal phrase draws meaning from the other part of the sentence and thus expresses a full idea. Second, though it does not have a connective word to express it, the verbal phrase does express the relationship of cause-and-result between the two full ideas—the accomplishing is the cause and the cancelling is the result.

SIMPLE SENTENCES: Peter wanted to finish the garage in three weeks. He had to work evenings as well as days.

VERBAL PHRASE: **To finish the garage in three weeks,** Peter had to work evenings as well as days.

Note again that even without a connective word (such as *because*), the verb phrase expresses a cause-and-result relationship between the two full ideas.

26A9 Absolute Phrases

An absolute phrase is a construction that has a subject with a nonfinite verb form (that is, a verb form that cannot serve as a sentence verb). Naturally such a phrase contains a full idea. Example:

SIMPLE SENTENCES: The dam burst. The residents of the canyon fled helter-skelter.
ABSOLUTE PHRASE: **The dam having burst,** the residents of the canyon fled helter-skelter.

As in all our illustrations in Section 26A, the *maturity* of the structure of the single sentence, as opposed to the simple sentences, should be clear to you.

26A10 Complex Sentences in General

As we said, no writer thinks about grammatical labels as he or she writes, but the good writer does think about composing sentences of mature structure, even though they may frequently be short, simple sentences. All of the sentence expansions we have illustrated can be combined in an infinity of ways to produce an infinity of different, but well-formed, English sentences. An example from an issue of *Harper's* magazine:

COMPLEX SENTENCE: When, like today, something moves me to get on the Fifth Avenue bus, my eyes invariably fall on one woman who seems, at least to me, the quintessential East Side woman, and her Martian differences quicken in me a sense of myself, a pang of self-recognition.

Though this complex sentence cannot really be called a typical sentence from *Harper's,* it is by no means unusual, and any page from that magazine or any other of good quality will contain many sentences of as much complexity. Good readers expect such sentences in their good reading material. In addition to two independent clauses, the sentence also contains one adverb clause, one adjective clause, two prepositional-phrase sentence modifiers, and one appositive as sentence expansions.

26B   EFFECTIVE SUBORDINATION

Avoid weak coordination of independent clauses; achieve effective subordination.

Sometimes two full ideas in one sentence are of equal importance and deserve equal emphasis, in which case they are usually coordinated. Examples, with the coordinated constituents in boldface:

PROPER COORDINATION: **At the outset we had foolishly envisioned immediate success,** but **after ten weeks of concentrated effort we were ready to quit.**

PROPER COORDINATION: **Having tried various experiments** and **having failed in each,** we had not even completed a prototype.

In the first sentence, two independent clauses are coordinated with the coordinating conjunction *but* joining them. In the second, two verbal phrases are coordinated. In each case the ideas, for effective sentence structure, deserve to be coordinated, or placed in equal rank.

Sometimes, one idea should, for effective sentence structure, be subordinated to another, for coordination of them makes the sentence sound childish. Examples:

WEAK COORDINATION: I had to carry all my books in my backpack every day, and it soon became quite heavy.

PROPER SUBORDINATION: **Since I had to carry all my books in my backpack every day,** it soon became quite heavy.

WEAK COORDINATION: The wound was quite deep, and it healed quickly.

PROPER SUBORDINATION: **Although the wound was quite deep,** it healed quickly.

The word *and* often produces weak coordination. Furthermore, the two ideas in each of the examples are not of equal importance. In the sentences of proper subordination, the boldface adverb clauses carry important meaning, but their subordination to the main clauses makes the sentences sound right—makes them more effective.

26C EMPHASIS

Compose sentences so that the most important ideas in them receive the most emphasis. Cultivate the active voice.

Choosing effective words (Chapters 20 to 22) and subordinating properly are two ways to achieve emphasis. A third method is to place the most prominent idea at the end of the sentence. Note this example from student writing.

UNEMPHATIC: Teenagers often have disagreements with their parents and the main reason is that the parents are afraid that their children will behave as *they* did when young and they therefore unreasonably restrict their children's behavior.

This sentence has an interesting idea but its parts are strung out in such a way that no peak of emphasis emerges. A revision:

EMPHATIC: Since many parents are afraid that their teenage children will behave as *they* did in their teens, they unreasonably restrict their children's behavior, thereby causing disagreements.

Now all three ideas still appear, but "causing disagreements" (even though it is not the independent clause) receives the most prominence because of its position at the end of the sentence.

Another example:

UNEMPHATIC: We won the game by a point, though with six minutes left we were down twelve points and down sixteen at half time.

The sentence is unemphatic because it winds down and ends with the least important information. A revision:

EMPHATIC: Though at half time we were down by sixteen points and with six minutes to go we were still down by twelve, we won the game by one point.

Now the use of subordination and the placement of the main idea at the end of the sentence combine to produce proper emphasis.

The passive voice is a proper grammatical construction, but the active voice produces a more effective style. Do not use the passive if there is no special reason to do so. Example:

UNEMPHATIC: Our canoe was capsized by our rivals and so the race was won by them.

EMPHATIC: Our rivals capsized our canoe and so won the race.

The passive voice weakens the first sentence, but the active voice in the revision produces proper emphasis.

26D CLARITY

Above all, be sure that what you have written will be clear to the reader.

In many sections of this book we have discussed writing problems that diminish clarity, and we will not discuss those writing problems a second time. However, it is just such problems—from inappropriate word choice to faulty sentence structure—that lead to confusion. Here is yet another example of lack of clarity, taken from a nationally circulated magazine:

LACK OF CLARITY: Every animal has its place and role in nature's grand design, including the predator. Ecological balance is one of nature's laws. Occasional loss of livestock must be weighed against the good *these animals* [italics supplied] do.

Most readers would be at least momentarily confused when they reached *these animals.* At first a reader may think the phrase refers to *livestock,* but that makes no sense. Eventually, it becomes clear that the phrase refers to *the predator,* but the damage of unclear writing has already been done. Besides, *predator* is singular and *these animals* plural, an inconsistency that contributes to the lack of clarity.

VARIETY

For more effectiveness in your writing, vary your sentence structure as you compose your paragraphs.

A series of sentences similar in structure, particularly if they are all short, produces monotonous writing. Note in the following example how the author uses the same sentence pattern throughout: "He thinks . . . He doesn't . . . He doesn't . . . He took . . . The doctor came . . . My father accepted . . . ." You can avoid such monotony by changing length, by using different kinds of sentence expansions (Section 26A), by beginning with elements other than the subject, and by occasionally using inverted word order—as the revision demonstrates.

MONOTONOUS SENTENCE STRUCTURE: My father was most disturbed by my brief period of experimenting with drugs. He thinks all drugs are bad. He doesn't understand why young people want to experiment. He doesn't remember the pleasure of getting high once in a while. He took me to our doctor to discuss the problem. The doctor came to the conclusion that I had no problem now. My father accepted the doctor's conclusion.

VARIETY IN SENTENCE STRUCTURE: Though I gave him concern about various of my activities, my father was most disturbed by my experimenting with drugs, especially since he thinks all drugs are bad. He is old enough now not to understand why young people want to experiment, and he evidently has forgotten the pleasure (which I am sure he experienced) of getting high once in a while. Because of his concern about my brief use of drugs, he went with me to discuss the problem with our family doctor. The doctor, having a much better knowledge of young people than my father, quickly explained that I now had no problem that should worry my father. Upon hearing this, my father breathed a sigh of relief and showed his old trust in me.

The monotony of the original is eliminated by the variety of sentence structure in the revision.

26F TRANSITIONS AND COHERENCE

Use connectives effectively both within and between sentences.

Essentially, writing consists of strings of ideas, and relationships exist between these ideas. Often there is no word between sentences or parts of a sentence to express a relationship; the relationship is clear simply because of the nature of the writing. Example:

> Growing weary with his team's many mistakes, the coach called off the practice session.

The cause-and-result relationship between the two sentence parts is fully clear even though the sentence has no specific word to express the relationship: the growing weary is the cause and the calling off is the result.

However, in addition to the coherence expressed by the sentence structure itself, our language has many connective words (coordinating conjunctions, subordinating conjunctions, and conjunctive adverbs) and transitional phrases (*for example, in addition, on the other hand,* and so on) that make clear the relationships between parts of sentences and between sentences. Good writers use such connectives wisely and liberally. The great English writer Samuel Taylor Coleridge said, "A good writer may be known by his pertinent use of connectives." And another great English writer, Thomas de Quincy, said, "All fluent and effective composition depends on the connectives." So be aware of connectives and use them effectively. Connectives provide **transition** between ideas, which in turn helps produce **coherence** in writing. Coherence means that all parts of each sentence and all sentences in a passage stick together, making the writing clear, intelligible, and smooth.

Some examples from student writing:

POOR TRANSITION: The world has much good in it. If I were given the ability to make it better, I would take three steps.

CLEAR TRANSITION: The world has much good in it, **but** if I were given the ability to make it better, I would take three steps.

CLEAR TRANSITION: **Though** the world has much good in it, it could be better. **Consequently,** if I were given the ability to improve it, I would take three steps.

POOR TRANSITION: Today's world is moving at a tremendous pace. That pace produces many pressures in everyday living. There are many ways to relieve them.

CLEAR TRANSITION: **Though** today's world produces tensions **because** it is moving at a tremendous pace, there are many ways to relieve the pressures of everyday living.

POOR TRANSITION: For a change of pace, a person can read the sports page. The rest of the paper should not be ignored.

CLEAR TRANSITION: For a change of pace, a person can read the sports page, **but** one should not ignore the rest of the paper.

CLEAR TRANSITION: **Though** reading the sports page can give a person a change of pace, one should not ignore the rest of the paper.

The boldface connective words in the sentences labeled *clear transition* express the relationships between ideas, relationships that are not expressed in the sentences labeled *poor transition.* Achieving clear transition through proper use of connectives is one way good writers make their writing coherent, which means that the sentences and parts of sentences flow smoothly together.

26G   LOGICAL THINKING

Avoid sweeping generalizations; strive for logical thinking.

Of course people are entitled to their own opinions (at least as long as they do not let them harm others), and a composition teacher certainly should not grade a paper down because he or she disagrees with the ideas in it. However, human beings often fall into illogical thinking. When you have written an illogical sentence or passage, your teacher should mark the faulty logic.

The most common kind of illogical statement that appears in themes is the **sweeping generalization,** a gross overstatement of the truth of whatever idea is under discussion. Example:

SWEEPING GENERALIZATION: All students everywhere today are again giving serious attention to their studies and avoiding political activism.

That might seem to be an innocent-enough sentence to appear in a theme, but its logic is faulty because the statement is too broad. It includes all students everywhere, and surely there are many students who are not giving serious attention to their studies and surely there are still many students who are politically active. Omitting the words *all* and *everywhere* would already modify the generalization somewhat by implying that the statement is true of only some.

MODIFIED STATEMENT: Students today are again giving serious attention to their studies and avoiding political activism.

Such sweeping generalizations need qualifications, which means the addition of words so as not to overstate the case or include everybody when not everybody should be included.

QUALIFIED GENERALIZATION: **A great many** students today in **most parts of the country** are again giving serious attention to their studies and avoiding political activism.

Now the qualifying words *a great many* and *most* take the statement out of the sweeping generalization category. Generalizations are not out of place in college writing. They appear each time you write a topic sentence for a paragraph or for a whole essay and thus assert the point you wish to make. But you cannot use a generalization— certainly not a sweeping generalization!—to support your argument. For that, you need either specific facts or clear logic or both.

A good course in logic will help you develop habits of clear thinking. As it does so, it will point out additional fallacies to avoid. In the meantime, try to use sound reasoning in all your writing, avoiding such illogic as in the following sentence:

ILLOGICAL: The press should not have treated the Republicans so harshly, because the Democrats were up to just as many dirty tricks.

Now even if the second part of the sentence is true, the whole is still illogical because one group's wrongdoing does not justify another group's wrongdoing. If the Democrats were guilty of crimes during the period the student referred to, they too should have been prosecuted and punished for their wrongdoing. The student would have been much more logical had he written his sentence in this way:

LOGICAL: Though the wrongdoings of the Republicans cannot be condoned, there is evidence of Democratic wrongdoing at the same time, and the Democrats certainly should have been castigated for their crimes too. It is not right for the press to turn all its attention to the crimes of just one party.

Human beings are prone to illogical thinking, but you can make the content of your papers sound if you give thought to the logic of the statements you make.

SECTION SIX

THE
RESEARCH
PAPER

27

The Research Paper

27A THE NATURE OF THE RESEARCH PAPER

Term papers are routinely assigned in many college courses, for studying a limited topic in depth is an especially valuable educational experience. In most colleges, the freshman course in composition has traditionally been the place to teach students the standardized, step-by-step techniques of preparing a research paper—techniques that are applicable to the various kinds of term papers assigned in more advanced college courses. In preparing a research paper, you will do practical research in a library, not original research, for you will be expected to seek out recorded knowledge, not to establish new knowledge.

Yet a research paper should be original in the sense that it puts together pieces of information from various sources in order to present a new view of a topic. For example, most people know that Roman Catholics in general oppose abortion on demand and that Protestants are split on the issue. But what is the view of Orthodox Jewish rabbis? Are they in general agreement, and if so, on which side? Or is there controversy among them on the issue of abortion? Perhaps no one has brought together in one article the statements from various sources detailing the Jewish position on abortion, and thus the topic might be a good one for a research paper. The writer of the paper would gather information from many sources and organize it into a research paper that would, in a sense, be new and original even though it used only recorded information.

The work of preparing a research paper ordinarily follows certain steps. These, listed first in summary form, are treated in detail in the remainder of this section.

Select a limited research-paper topic.
Become generally acquainted with the topic.
If possible, construct a tentative broad outline.
Build a working bibliography.
Read and take notes.
Construct a full outline.
Write the first draft, incorporating citations.
Revise and edit as necessary.
Prepare the final manuscript.
Proofread and submit on time.

It will be helpful to read Chapter 27 entirely before you begin actual work on your paper.

27B SELECTING A LIMITED RESEARCH-PAPER TOPIC

A freshman research paper normally runs between 2000 and 3000 words, and thus its topic must be rather narrowly limited, for a broad or general topic cannot be well developed in so few words. Students who try to write papers on such topics as "Scandals in the Nixon Administration," "The Vietnam War," and "Shakespeare's Tragedies" are hopelessly lost at the beginning. After you decide on the general subject you want to write about, you must go through a process of reducing and reducing that subject until you reach a properly limited topic.

Often, reading an article or news story about the general subject you are interested in will lead you to a narrow topic. For example, one student, after reading a news article about Uri Geller, an Israeli who claims to have various psychic powers, decided she wanted to write her paper on some aspect of psychic phenomena. She realized that such topics as "Extrasensory Perception" and "Psychokinesis" were much too broad. She considered "Scientific Experiments in Extrasensory Perception," but also rejected that topic as too broad. Then a minor comment in the news article led her to the properly limited topic "Controls Used to Prevent Fraud in Experiments in Extrasensory Perception." You must, then, proceed from a general subject to a narrow aspect of it in order to select a properly limited research-paper topic.

But a narrowly limited topic is not necessarily a good research-paper topic, for a good research paper must bring together information from at least eight or ten sources. *Thus any topic for which you can find sufficient materials in only one, two, or three sources is not an acceptable research-paper topic.*

Some good research-paper topics call only for the presentation of factual, noncontroversial information; others are on controversial issues. If, for example, you are interested in mental illness and choose the topic "Some Rare Types of Mental Illness," you would gather factual information and present it in an orderly and interesting fashion. But if you should choose the topic "The Use of Chemical Therapy in Minor Cases of Mental Illness," you would find much disagreement among the experts as to whether, or how much, chemical therapy should be used to treat minor mental illnesses. You would, in effect, have a controversial topic. After studying the evidence, you would put your own conclusions in your paper. True, your conclusions are opinions, but much of your paper will consist of the facts on which you base those opinions.

After you have a suitable topic, you should, before compiling a working bibliography (see Section 27D), try to decide what the main points of your paper will be. The more clearly you perceive your topic before beginning your research, the easier your research will be and the less time you will waste. Of course, before beginning your research you may know very little about your topic, but if you can establish the main questions your paper will answer, you will have a good head start.

The reading you do to narrow your topic (encyclopedia articles, news stories, articles in journals and magazines) will also help you construct a broad general outline by suggesting such questions.

Suppose, for example, you chose the topic "The Use of Hypnosis as an Anesthetic." You would probably look for answers to these questions: How widespread is the use of hypnosis as an anesthetic? On what kinds of patients and for what kinds of surgery is it used? How much success do the doctors who use it claim? Is there much professional opposition to its use? With these few questions in mind (they would become main headings in your outline), you would have a great advantage in beginning and pursuing your research.

27C RESEARCH MATERIALS IN THE LIBRARY

After you have selected a good topic and, if possible, derived from it the few general questions your paper will answer, your next step is to compile a working bibliography. This is a list of sources (books, magazine articles, news reports, and so on) that you expect to provide all the information you will need to write your paper. To compile a working bibliography, you must know what source materials are available and how to use them. Thus in the following sections we will classify the chief library research materials, so that you will be equipped to compile a working bibliography. Every good library has at least one reference librarian on duty whenever the library is open, and you should not hesitate to call on the reference librarian for help. Also, your composition instructor may take his or her class on a tour of your library.

27C1 General and Special Encyclopedias and Reference Books

Every library of any size has many general and specialized reference works, which are kept on open shelves in the library's reference room. Since these reference works are themselves the product of research, they alone cannot supply you with all the information you need for a good research paper. Remember, especially when contemplating the use of a general encyclopedia, that when one source supplies you with all the information you need for your research paper, you do not have a suitable topic. Nevertheless, the various reference works often supply researchers with useful bits of information, and you should consult them as necessary. For example, if you should choose the topic "Critical Reception of Mark Twain's Satires on Religion," *The Dictionary of American Biography* might provide you with some useful bits of background information about Mark Twain, though it could by no means supply you with sufficient materials to write the whole paper.

The two most important general encyclopedias are the *Encyclopedia Americana* and the *Encyclopaedia Britannica.* (An article in these works is sometimes followed by a bibliography, which may list useful sources.) Listed below, by subject, are the most widely used specialized reference works. Your library will probably have most of these, in addition to many lesser known reference books that there is not space to list here.

Agriculture
Encyclopedia of American Agriculture, 4 vols.

Art and Architecture
Cyclopedia of Painters and Paintings, 4 vols.
Encyclopedia of World Art
A History of Architecture

Biography
American Men and Women of Science, 11 vols.
Contemporary Authors, 52 vols.
Current Biography, 34 vols.
Dictionary of American Biography, 20 vols. and supplements
Dictionary of National Biography (British), 22 vols. and supplements
Who's Who (British)
Who's Who in America

Business
Economic Almanac, 34 vols.
Encyclopedia of Banking and Finance

Education
Cyclopedia of Education, 5 vols.
Education Index, monthly, with annual cumulations
Encyclopedia of Educational Research

History
Cambridge Ancient History, 12 vols.
Cambridge Modern History, 13 vols.
Dictionary of American History, 6 vols.
An Encyclopedia of World History
Shorter Cambridge Medieval History, 2 vols.

Literature
Cambridge History of American Literature, 4 vols.
Cambridge History of English Literature, 15 vols.
Cassell's Encyclopedia of World Literature, 2 vols.
Encyclopedia of Classical Mythology
Granger's Index to Poetry
Mythology of All Races, 13 vols.
Oxford Companion to American Literature
Oxford Companion to Classical Literature
Oxford Companion to English Literature

Music
> *Grove's Dictionary of Music and Musicians,* 9 vols. and supplement
> *Musician's Guide,* 3 vols.

Political Science
> *Cyclopedia of American Government,* 3 vols.
> *Dictionary of Political Science*
> *Palgrave's Dictionary of Political Economy,* 3 vols.

Religion
> *Encyclopedia of Religion and Ethics,* 13 vols.
> *Encyclopedia of the Jewish Religion*
> *Interpreter's Dictionary of the Bible,* 4 vols.
> *New Catholic Encyclopedia,* 14 vols.

Science
> *The Harper Encyclopedia of Science*
> *Hutchinson's Technical and Scientific Encyclopedia,* 4 vols.
> *McGraw-Hill Encyclopedia of Science and Technology,* 15 vols.

Social Science
> *Dictionary of Philosophy and Psychology,* 3 vols.
> *Encyclopedia of Psychology*
> *Encyclopedia of the Social Sciences,* 15 vols.

Yearbooks
> *The Americana Annual*
> *The Britannica Book of the Year*
> *Statesman's Yearbook*
> *United Nations Yearbook*
> *World Almanac*

Don't hesitate to use any of these or other reference works to obtain useful bits of information and to verify facts, but *do not* expect to write a research paper using only reference works of this sort.

27C2   The Card Catalogue

A library's card catalogue lists, alphabetically, all the books and pamphlets in the library's holdings. To facilitate research, each book is listed at least three times: (1) under the author's name; (2) under its title; and (3) under one or more subject headings. Occasionally a college researcher will know the name of an author who has written on the researcher's topic but will not remember any of that author's titles. And occasionally the researcher may remember a title but not its author. Thus the listings by author and title can be useful. But most researchers rely mainly on subject headings to guide them to useful books and pamphlets. Here is a reproduction of a card entered in the card catalogue by subject heading:

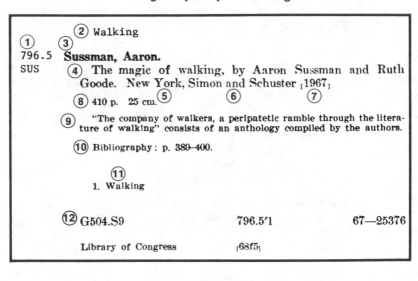

The encircled numbers do not appear on the card in its file. They correspond to the following explanations:

(1) Library call number

(2) Subject heading

(3) Author

(4) Title

(5) Place of publication

(6) Publisher

(7) Date of publication

(8) Length and size of book

(9) Statement by author or publisher

(10) 12-page bibliography in book

(11) Subject heading

(12) Information for librarians

The above book, with the same information about it, is also entered in the card catalogue under "Sussman, Aaron," under "Goode, Ruth," and under "The Magic of Walking," this last being alphabetized under the M's.

27C3   Cross-References

Even after you understand how books are entered three times in the card catalogue, you may still feel insecure in doing research. You may not know any authors or titles that will provide you with useful information, and you may not know what subject heading to look under. Suppose, for example, you had seen the recent headline "Why 26,000,000 Johnnies Can't Read" and had become curious as to why so many Americans are functionally illiterate. You might eventually decide on the topic "Some Controversial Methods of Teaching First-Graders to Read." What subject heading would you look under? You might well feel baffled and frustrated. But the standardized techniques of library research come to your aid.

First you canvass your mind for subject headings that might possibly be in the card catalogue and jot them down: "Reading," "Teaching Reading," "Teaching Methods" or "Methodology," "Phonics," "Look-Say Method," "Progressive Education," "Elementary Education," "Reading Readiness," and so on. Chances are high that at least one subject heading you thought of will be in the card catalogue. Then cross-references will come to your rescue. Most subject headings have a cross-reference card that lists various related headings. These cross-reference cards come *after* all the cards listing books under a particular subject heading, and they begin with "See also." For example, in one card catalogue, after a large number of books having the subject heading "Political Science," there are twelve cross-reference cards listing about one hundred subject headings, ranging from "Administrative Law" to "World Politics." Some subjects will have many cross-references; some may have very few. But learning to use cross-references is an essential part of learning to write research papers.

27C4   The Periodical Indexes

Periodical literature is that which is published at regular intervals: daily, weekly, biweekly, monthly, and so on. The hundreds and hundreds of reputable magazines and learned journals that have been published in the past or that are still being published are rich sources of information for writers of research papers. In fact, many topics—especially ones on contemporary issues or events—will send the researcher only to magazine articles, rather than to reference works and the card catalogue. To facilitate a researcher's use of the various magazines, all good libraries purchase cumulative periodical indexes, which list articles that have appeared in all the periodicals that any one index chooses as its domain. Articles are listed twice: by author and by subject heading.

For the freshman composition student who is learning to prepare a research paper, the most useful periodical index, by far, is *The Reader's Guide to Periodical Literature,* which lists articles from about 200 widely circulated magazines. The *Guide* begins at 1900 and covers many good magazines now defunct. About every ten to twelve weeks a small volume of the *Guide* appears, and the small volumes are then combined into large volumes that list articles for one or two years. All the volumes of the *Guide* are always kept on open shelves in a library's reference room.

The list on the facing page is a sample of listings from *The Reader's Guide,* with an explanation of the first entry. The author's last name and the subject headings are in boldface capitals. The title of each article is given in full. All abbreviations are clearly explained in the preface of each volume of the *Guide.* The first entry in the sample on page 255 refers to an illustrated article in *Popular Science,* volume 206, pages 108–10 and continued, February 1975.

Cross-references (such as that under "Sole") are as important in *The Reader's Guide* as they are in the card catalogue. For example, there are twenty-six cross-references for the subject heading "Literature" in one volume of the *Guide,* ranging from "Authorship" to "Symbolism in Literature." Remember, cross-references are extremely important to researchers.

"illustrated"   volume   pages   month and year

SOLAR heating
How to trap solar heat with your windows. E. Allen. il Pop Sci 206:108-10+ F '75
Now you buy solar heating equipment for your home. R. Stepler. il Pop Sci 206:74-7+ Mr '75
Solar heating study. il Chemistry 48:4 F '75
Sun power. P. Gwynne. il Newsweek 85:50+ F 24 '75
SOLAR-MEC (Munters environmental control) unit. See Air conditioning equipment
SOLAR observatories. See Astronomical observatories
SOLAR radiation
Variable star. Sci Am 232:49 Mr '75
  See also
Solar heating
Solar wind
SOLAR system
Most primitive objects in the solar system; carbonaceous chondrites. L. Grossman. il Sci Am 232:30-8 bibl(p 114) F '75
Rubidium-87/strontium-87 age of Juvinas basaltic achondrite and early igneous activity in the solar system. C. J. Allègre and others. bibl il Science 187:436-8 F 7 '75
Velikovsky: paradigms in collision. G. Kolodity. bibl il Bull Atom Sci 31:36-8 F '75
  See also
Planets
SOLAR wind
Electron microscopy of irradiation effects in space. M. Maurette and P. B. Price. bibl il Science 187:121-9 Ja 17 '75
Solar nitrogen: evidence for a secular increase in the ratio of nitrogen-15 to nitrogen-14. J. F. Kerridge. bibl il Science 188:162-4 Ap 11 '75
SOLE (fish)
  See also
Cookery—Fish
SOLETA, Justin A.
Education of the Amish. Educ Digest 40:48-50 Ja '75
SOLID wastes. See Refuse and refuse disposal
SOLLID, John
East Sequim bay; poem. Nation 220:473 Ap 19 '75
SOLOMON, Goody L.
Help for house hazards. Read Digest 106:177-8+ Mr '75
SOLOMON, Leslie
Power surges and semiconductors. Pop Electr 7:42 F '75
SOLTI, Sir Georg
Americanization of Sir Georg Solti. R. C. Marsh. il Sat R 2:38-40+ Ap 19 '75 •
SOLVENTS
  See also
Cleaning compositions

Other periodical indexes sometimes of use to beginning researchers are the following:

Art Index (from 1929)

Biography Index (from 1946)

Biological and Agricultural Index (includes books, pamphlets, and articles, from 1916)

Book Review Digest (lists book reviews by author, title, and subject, from 1905)

Dramatic Index (American and British, from 1909)

Education Index (includes books, pamphlets, and articles, from 1929)

Engineering Index (from 1884)

Index to Legal Periodicals (from 1926)

Industrial Arts Index (from 1913)

Poole's Index to Periodical Literature (covers American and British periodicals, most now defunct, from 1802 to 1906)

Public Affairs Information Service (covers books, periodicals, and pamphlets in economics, government, and public affairs, from 1915)

Quarterly Cumulative Index Medicus (covers medical literature, from 1927)

Social Science and Humanities Index (covers American and foreign periodicals, from 1907)

United States Government Publications (from 1895)

Most large libraries will have most of these indexes.

One other index that often is very useful is the *New York Times Index,* published monthly with annual volumes since 1913. It indexes all important news stories, editorials, and feature articles that appear in the *New York Times,* giving not only the location of the article but also a brief summary of it. Thus if your topic is one that at some time has been newsworthy—such as "The Entrapment of the Egyptian Third Army in the Yom Kippur War"—you can look in the *New York Times Index* for 1973 and find the location and brief summaries of news reports that will furnish useful information. Even if your library does not have copies of past issues of the *New York Times,* the *Index* is still helpful, for other daily newspapers would be likely to have had news stories similar to those in the *New York Times* that were published on the same day.

27C5   The Periodical Card File

The periodical indexes are useful to you, of course, only when your library has a copy of the magazine you want. So that researchers can quickly find out whether particular issues of particular magazines are available, most large libraries have a periodical card file, which is located in the reference room and which lists the issues of all magazines the library has in its holdings. Smaller libraries sometimes enter the periodical cards alphabetically in the card catalogue, and some keep at the reference desk or checkout counter a typed list of all magazines in their holdings. Usually the magazines themselves are bound in volumes of six issues or more, with the inclusive dates printed on the spines, and are shelved alphabetically in the reference room. Libraries with large holdings often have old issues of magazines in storage and will make them available on request.

27D   COMPILING A WORKING BIBLIOGRAPHY

A bibliography is a list of books, articles, and perhaps other source materials, such as television tapes, on a particular topic such as "Shakespeare" or "Shakespeare's Comedies" or "Shakespeare's *Twelfth Night.*" The bibliography of your research paper will be a list of all the sources you used in preparing your paper. A working bibliography is a preliminary list of sources that you *hope* will provide you with useful information. It is standard practice for a researcher to compile as complete a working bibliography as possible *before* he or she begins reading sources and taking notes. Four points are of especial importance here: (1) If you have been able to derive from your topic the few general questions you expect your paper to answer (see Section 27B), you will be much less likely to enter useless sources in your working bibliography. (2) If a useful book listed in the card catalogue contains a bibliography (see Section 27C2), it is helpful to check that book out at once and use its bibliography. (3) Be especially careful to make full use of cross-references in both the card catalogue and *The Reader's Guide.* And (4) after you have compiled a working bibliography and have begun reading and taking notes, watch for other sources that you can add to your working bibliography. Thus the working bibliography is fluid, not static. You will probably drop from it sources that turn out not to be useful, and you will probably add to it after you begin reading your source materials.

Standard procedure calls for listing bibliographic entries on 3" x 5" cards. You *never* enter more than one source on one card. In the upper right-hand corners, number each card consecutively; having the cards numbered will let you identify the sources of your notes (see Section 27F1) by number rather than by authors and titles. Be certain to enter on each bibliography card all essential information about the book or article; failure to enter complete information will cost you much wasted time in rechecking when you are ready to obtain materials from the library and when you write footnotes and prepare the formal bibliography for your paper. (If one or more bits of information are not available when you first make up the card for your working bibliography, be sure to add those items to the card when you begin to read in that source.)

Put on separate lines on each bibliography card all the

following items of information that are applicable (some apply only to books; some only to magazine articles):

(1) the library call number of a book or periodical
(2) the full name of the author (last name first)
(3) the exact title of the item (underlined or in quotation marks)
(4) the place of publication, the publisher, and the date of publication
(5) the exact name of a magazine
(6) the date and volume number (if any) of a magazine and the pages on which the article appears
(7) the name and volume number of any reference work, the title of the article, and the pages on which the article appears
(8) a note as to whether the item has a bibliography of its own or some other feature, such as illustrations, that may be useful to you

All this information (except 7) can be obtained from the card catalogue or *The Reader's Guide;* you need not check out materials from the library to compile a working bibliography. *The value of following this standard procedure cannot be overemphasized.*
    Here is a sample bibliography card:

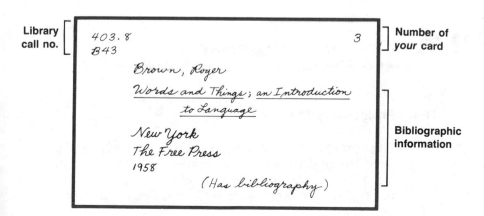

Library call no.

403.8
B43   3

Number of *your* card

Brown, Roger
Words and Things; an Introduction to Language

New York
The Free Press
1958
            (Has bibliography)

Bibliographic information

And a card for a magazine article:

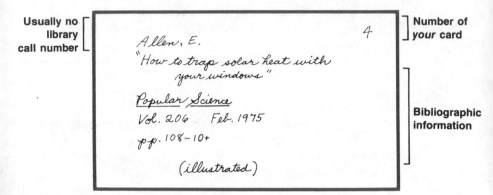

Usually no
library
call number

Number of
your card

Bibliographic
information

Allen, E.
"How to trap solar heat with
*   your windows"*

Popular Science
Vol. 206   Feb. 1975
pp. 108–10+

(illustrated)

4

A bibliography card with complete information will allow
you to write footnotes and the entry in the formal bibliography without consulting the card catalogue or *The Reader's Guide* again. Also, numbering the cards 1, 2, 3, and
so on, will let you indicate on your note cards where your
information came from without having to write the title and
author on the note card itself.

27E OUTLINING: PRELIMINARY
AND FORMAL

27E1 Preliminary Outlining

The next step after compiling a working bibliography is to
make, as best you can, a preliminary, scratch outline of
the main points (Roman-numeral headings) of your
paper. If, as you were advised to do in Section 27B, you

have derived from your topic the few general questions you expect your paper to answer, you can make a serviceable preliminary outline. For example, if you should select the topic "Charles Dickens's Reactions to America and Americans," you might begin with this preliminary outline:

I. The number of and reasons for Dickens's trips to America
II. His reactions to the social structure of America
III. His reactions to the geography and climate of America.
IV. His contacts with and reactions to notable American writers

Even with this slight preliminary outline, your task of scanning and reading your source materials for useful information will be far easier than if you begin reading and taking notes with no plan in mind. Also, with such a preliminary outline you can indicate by Roman numerals on your note cards where the information on them will fit in your paper. As you read and take notes, you should revise your preliminary outline as seems appropriate, perhaps adding subheadings.

27E2 Formal Outlining

A preliminary, or scratch, outline, which need not observe all the principles of formal outlining, is for the writer's use; but a formal outline is for the reader. After you have read the material and taken notes, you should prepare a more complete outline to help you write the first draft and to include, after revision, with your final copy. Your instructor may specify either a topic outline (in which the headings are phrases) or a sentence outline. Example:

TOPIC OUTLINE: Faulkner's association with Sherwood Anderson in New Orleans
SENTENCE OUTLINE: Faulkner associated with Sherwood Anderson in New Orleans.

In the rest of this section, illustrations will be of the topic-outline kind.

Your formal outline should observe the following six principles of good outlining:

(1) Your outline should be properly balanced. It should not consist only of a few Roman-numeral headings, and it probably should not have headings below the third level. For a 2500-word paper, an outline usually should consist of only two or three levels. Don't make outline headings out of specific details.

(2) Make your outline headings meaningful. Example:

MEANINGLESS HEADINGS: I. Introduction
                              II. Newspaper work
MEANINGFUL HEADINGS: I. Mark Twain's arrival in Nevada
                              II. His first full-time job as a newspaper reporter.

(3) Be sure your headings are parallel in content. All the Roman-numeral headings should be divisions of the title or topic; all the capital-letter headings should be divisions of Roman-numeral headings; and so on. Example:

FAULTY PARALLELISM   I. Patton's sensational behavior
  OF CONTENT: A. His slapping a soldier
                        B. His leaking security information to the press
               II. His attempt to start a war with Russia

For parallelism of content, Roman numeral II should be C under Roman numeral I, for it is a division of that heading, not of the topic.

(4) Keep your headings parallel in structure. In a sentence outline no problem exists, but in a topic outline all the headings in any one division and level should have the same grammatical structure. Example:

FAULTY PARALLELISM   I. The critics' first reaction to *The*
  OF STRUCTURE: *Waste Land*
               II. Coming to understand its symbolic meaning

A noun phrase and a verb phrase are in faulty parallelism. For proper parallelism of structure, Roman numeral II should be a noun phrase too:

PROPER PARALLELISM: II. The critics' later recognition of the symbolic meaning of *The Waste Land*

(5) Do not use single subheadings except to list examples. Example:

WRONG: I. Emerson's reaction to Whitman's poetry
           A. Favorably impressed
    II. James Russell Lowell's reaction to Whitman's poetry

The heading A should simply be incorporated into Roman numeral I, perhaps as "Emerson's favorable reaction to Whitman's poetry."

RIGHT: I. The initial success of the Head Start program
          A. Example: Results in the Grace Bird Elementary School
    II The first expansion of the Head Start program

(6) Whatever your method of punctuation and of numbering headings, be consistent.

27F NOTE-TAKING AND SOME RELATED PROBLEMS

After you have compiled a working bibliography and have prepared as much of a preliminary outline as you can, your next step is to begin reading or scanning your sources to find information useful for your paper. Since you cannot remember all that you read, you must take notes, which should be written on 4″ x 6″ cards. Your reading may at first seem haphazard, but putting one idea on each card enables you later to arrange your information in a usable order. If your topic is on a controversial issue, evaluate your sources as best you can for reliability and completeness of information. Avoid articles that have a strong ring of propaganda to them, such as one that labels a respectable politician as either a communist or fascist. As you take notes, try to digest and assimilate your materials in order to understand your topic well; do not transfer information from a source to a note card without letting it pass through and make an impression on your mind.

27F1   Techniques of Note-taking

Follow these directions in taking notes: (1) Identify the source of your information with the number of its bibliography card. This will help you avoid repeated copying of titles and authors. (2) Never put information from two sources on one note card; each card should have just one bibliography-card number. (3) Enter on each note card the exact page numbers from which its information comes. This will prevent your having to recheck page numbers in case you need to footnote the information. (4) Using your preliminary outline, avoid putting on one note card two or more pieces of information that will fall under different Roman-numeral headings. As your preliminary outline develops, try to indicate on each card just which part of your paper the information on the card belongs in. (5) Learn to scan articles and chapters from books so that you can quickly tell whether a source has useful information for you. The fuller your preliminary outline, the more effectively you can scan for useful information. When you see that a source has information important to your paper, stop scanning and read carefully in order to take usable notes. (6) Take condensed or verbatim notes according to directions given in Sections 27F2 and 27F3.

Here is a sample note card, written for a paper entitled "The Purchase of Russian America":

I   5

> Quite clear why Russia wanted to sell Russian America. The territory was a burden. Produced no net income. Russian American Company bankrupt, wanting subsidies. Territory too far from seat of Russia's government. On verge of war with England and feared England might capture the territory. Needed money and felt it best to sell rather than risk total loss.
>
> pp. 21-22

The Arabic numeral 5 is the number of the bibliography card listing the source. The information, which is condensed, came from pages 21–22 of the source. The Roman numeral I indicates that this information belongs to the first main point of the paper.

27F2 Direct Quotations

Direct quotations have four uses in research papers: (1) to give the exact words of an authority in order to lend weight to a point of view; (2) to present original evidence as proof of a point; (3) to emphasize a fact or opinion; and (4) to share with the reader a passage that is striking because of its excellent style, wit, or some other feature. You should *not* use a direct quotation unless it clearly fulfills one of these purposes; do not aimlessly scatter quotations throughout your paper.

Quotations that occupy five or fewer lines of a typed paper should be incorporated into the paper with quotation marks. Quotations that are five lines or longer are called insets. They are indented five spaces, are double-spaced in term papers (but single-spaced in theses and dissertations [see the example on page 277]), and are *not* enclosed in quotation marks. Both such shorter and longer quotations are illustrated in Section 27H. Three spaced periods (. . .), called an ellipsis, indicate that part of a direct quotation has been omitted.

When, in taking notes, you think a passage might serve well in your paper as a direct quotation, put it on your note card verbatim and clearly indicate with quotation marks that it is the exact wording of the original. You may, of course, decide later not to use such a passage as a direct quotation. Don't overuse direct quotations.

When entering a direct quotation into your paper, lead smoothly into it with an introductory phrase or sentence that announces that a quotation is coming and indicates its purpose. For example, such a simple phrase as "According to the well-known cosmologist Fred Hoyle, . . ." can serve to introduce a quotation and tell the reader that an authority is being cited. Don't just use a direct quotation abruptly; announce it in some way.

27F3   Paraphrasing and Plagiarism

Since only a small part of your research paper will consist of direct quotations, most of your note-taking should not be verbatim but should be a condensed version of the information you expect to use. Thus as you take notes, use your own words as much as possible and compress the information so that you can re-expand it in your own words when you enter it into your paper. The process of using your own words instead of a direct quotation to incorporate source materials into your paper is known as paraphrasing. That is, you do not change the information but you do change the wording so that it is in your style and not the original author's. If you take condensed notes, paraphrasing will be much easier for you.

Failure to paraphrase is one of the deadly sins in research-paper writing, for it leads to plagiarism, which is literary theft, or pretending someone else's writing is yours. Many teachers fail research papers for plagiarism alone. Of course, since you are gathering your information from written sources, you must use some of the wording of the original, but you must not quote whole sentences and then, by not using quotation marks, pretend that you composed them. Even if you paraphrase, you can avoid the charge of plagiarism by giving credit to your source. A footnote or a phrase like "Betts states that . . ." will protect you. Your research paper, for the most part, must be of your own composition. Technical terms, statistics, and some phrasing must be as they are in the original source; but the structure of the sentences and much of the vocabulary must be yours. As a rough guide, try never to have in one sentence more than five consecutive words exactly as they appear in the original source (except, of course, for direct quotations).

27G DOCUMENTATION

Documentation in a research paper is the acknowledgment of the sources used. It includes footnotes and the formal bibliography.

27G1 Uses of Footnotes

In research papers, footnotes are used (1) to acknowledge the sources of direct quotations; (2) to acknowledge the sources of important paraphrased information that might be subject to question or that the reader might want to pursue further; and (3) to enter explanatory comments that would be out of place in the text of the paper. This third use is rare in freshman research papers.

Do *not* footnote (1) well-known quotations (such as those from the Bible); (2) ordinary dictionary definitions, unless one has some special purpose such as refuting widely accepted information; (3) simple and easily ascertainable facts, such as birth and death dates of a famous person; and (4) paraphrased information that a critical reader will accept without question and that is not of considerable importance to the main point of your paper.

27G2 Location of Footnotes

Some instructors prefer footnotes to be at the bottom of pages that have sources acknowledged, and some instructors prefer all the footnotes to be on a separate page, or pages, at the end of the research paper, but before the formal bibliography. The latter method is much easier for students who type their papers, but in Section 27H the bottom-of-the-page method is illustrated.

Follow these directions in entering footnotes in your paper: (1) In the text of your paper, put the footnote number immediately **after** the final quotation marks for a short quotation, at the end of an inset quotation, and at the end of a paraphrased passage of which you are acknowledging the source. (2) If an author's full name has been used in a footnoted passage, omit the name in the footnote if the footnote is at the bottom of the page. (3) Use raised numbers, not numbers followed by periods. In the footnote itself, leave one space between the raised number and the first letter of the note. (4) Number footnotes consecutively throughout the paper or, if your paper contains more than one chapter, throughout each chapter. (5) Indent each footnote as though it began a paragraph, that is, indent five spaces. (6) Single-space each footnote, but double-space between footnotes (or, if your instructor requires it, double-space both within and between footnotes). (7) When putting footnotes at the bottom of the page, quadruple-space between the last line of the text of your paper and the first line of the footnote. (Some instructors may require you to draw or type a two- or three-inch line between the text and the footnote, leaving a double space above and below the line.) And (8) be sure that each footnote has marks of punctuation and underlining exactly as the forms in Section 27G3 specify. Note the period that ends each footnote as if it were a sentence.

27G3   Footnote Forms

Following are footnote forms for every kind of source material you are likely to use in preparing your research paper. Some rare forms, such as one for a book with unnumbered pages, are omitted. These forms follow the *MLA Handbook for Writers* (1977), a publication of the Modern Language Association of America. In general, footnotes that identify sources contain three important bits of information: the author's name(s) in normal order, the work and its publication information, and the numbers of the pages where this particular item can be found. Note that footnotes for magazines and newspaper articles differ somewhat from those for books and pamphlets.

A book with one author:

[1] James Work, <u>Boswell's Youth</u> (New York: Vintage Press, 1972), p. 71.

A book with two or more authors:

[2] Rachel Foreman, Clive Sims, and Earl Bates, <u>English Politics in the 1780's</u> (Chicago: The Univ. of Chicago Press, 1974), pp. 204–05.

(Note: If there are more than three authors, name the first and add *et al.* in this manner: "George Witter et al. . . . ." *Et al.* means "and others.")

An edited collection, the editor being cited:

^{3} Norman Thomas, ed., <u>Essays on the Enlightenment</u> (Oxford: Clarendon Press, 1975), p. ix.

An edited work, the original author being cited:

^{4} James Boswell, <u>Journal of a Tour to the Hebrides</u>, ed. Thomas Parnell (Cambridge: Belknap Press, 1969), p. 108.

An edited collection, one of the authors being cited:

^{5} Edward Hooker, "Boswell's Phobias," in <u>Neoclassical Studies</u>, ed. John Putt (Los Angeles: Clark Press, 1962), pp. 116–17.

A work in several volumes:

^{6} Samuel Monk, <u>Johnson's Circle</u> (New York: Norton, 1971), II, 312.

(Note: When page numbers follow a volume number, the abbreviation *p.* or *pp.* is omitted.)

A translated work:

^{7} Klaus Brindle, <u>Political Poetry</u>, trans. H. T. More (New York: Random House, 1952), p. 92.

A later or revised edition:

^{8} W. A. Tuttle, <u>Boswell in Holland</u>, 2nd ed. (New York: Viking Press, 1973), p. 84.

A reference work:

[9] "Boswell, James," The Dictionary of
National Biography (London: Oxford Univ. Press,
1917), II, 896.

An anonymous pamphlet:

[10] Preparing Your Dissertation for
Microfilming (Ann Arbor, Mich.: University
Microfilms, n.d.), p. 4.

(**Note:** Signed pamphlets are footnoted just as books are. Also
n.d. = no date.)

An article from a learned journal:

[11] Michael Abrams, "Dr. Johnson's Poetry,"
College English, 30 (Jan. 1969), 267–68.

(**Note:** The 30 is the volume number.)

An article in a monthly magazine:

[12] Gary Puttle, "Boswell and Louisa," The
Atlantic, Sept. 1968, pp. 90–92.

An article in a weekly magazine:

[13] Norman Uncles, "Mr. Boswell and Dr.
Johnson," Saturday Review, 26 July 1969, pp.
21–22.

An unsigned article in a weekly magazine:

[14] "New Dirt on Boswell," Time, 4 July 1969,
p. 32.

Articles in newspapers:

[15] Robert Kirsh, "New Material on Boswell,"
The Los Angeles Times, 9 Nov. 1974, Sec. 3,
p. 26, cols. 2–4.

[16] "A New Boswell Scandal," The Spokesman
Review (Spokane, Wash.), 8 Jan. 1975, p. 12,
col. 3.

Subsequent references:

Once a work has been footnoted, subsequent references to it may be short forms. The *MLA Handbook* considers such abbreviations as *op. cit., loc. cit.,* and *ibid.* superfluous. Instead, use a short form reference that is clear and easily recognizable by your reader, usually the author's last name and the page number, as in footnote 19 below.

[17] James Work, Boswell's Youth (New York:
Vintage Press, 1972), p. 71.
[18] Samuel Monk, Johnson's Circle (New York:
Norton, 1971), II, 312.
[19] Monk, p. 317.
[20] James Work, Boswell as Lawyer (New York:
Norton, 1975), p. 121.

If (as in the case of James Work above) an author has more than one work cited, then the short form for each must include the last name of the author, the title (shortened, if convenient), and the page number. If a subsequent reference is to an anonymous work, the title and page number make a short form.

[21] Thomas, p. xi.
[22] Work, Boswell as Lawyer, p. 122.
[23] Work, Boswell's Youth, p. 73.
[24] "New Dirt on Boswell," p. 33.

27G4 Bibliographic Forms

At the end of your research paper you present a formal bibliography of the sources you have used. All bibliographic entries should be in one alphabetized list of authors' names. Note that their form differs from that of footnote entries and that you do not list only the pages you used but the entire work you consulted in each case. If a work is anonymous, alphabetize it by the title, but ignore *a*, *an*, and *the* as initial words. Authors' last names come first in bibliographic entries. If you list two or more entries for the same author, you may substitute a dash ten hyphens long on the typewriter (----------) for the name after its first use. Bibliographic entries are indented just the opposite of footnotes: the first line is flush left; the next line is indented five spaces. Single-space each bibliographic entry but double-space between entries (or, if your instructor requires it, double-space throughout). Do not number entries. Use the heading "Bibliography" centered two inches from the top of a new page, regardless of how much space is left on the preceding page. The following forms are modeled on those of the *MLA Handbook for Writers* (1977):

A book:

```
Foreman, Rachel, and Clive Sims.   Boswell's
     Politics.  New York:  Harcourt Brace
     Jovanovich, 1971.
```

(**Note:** If there is more than one author, only the first author's name is inverted.)

Two or more books by the same author:

```
Work, James.   Boswell's Youth.   New York:
     Vintage Press, 1972.
----------.   Boswell as Lawyer.   New York:
     Norton, 1975.
```

(**Note:** Works by the same author may be arranged chronologically, as above, or alphabetically by title.)

Edited books:

Essays on the Enlightenment. Ed. Norman Thomas.
Oxford: Clarendon Press, 1975.

or

Thomas, Norman, ed. Essays on the Enlightenment.
Oxford: Clarendon Press, 1975.

Boswell, James. Journal of a Tour to the
Hebrides. Ed. Thomas Parnell. Cambridge:
Belknap Press, 1969.

A work in several volumes:

Parker, W. O. Boswell: A Biography. 2 vols.
New York: Holt, Rinehart and Winston,
1973.

A translated work:

Brindle, Klaus, Political Poetry. Trans. H. T.
More. New York: Random House, 1952.

A later or revised edition:

Tuttle, W. A. Boswell in Holland. 2nd ed. New
York: Viking Press, 1973.

A reference work:

"Boswell, James." The Dictionary of National
Biography. London: Oxford Univ. Press, 1917.
II, 893–900.

An anonymous pamphlet:

English Political Morality. London: The Society
of Friends, 1968.

An article in a learned journal:

Hogg, Jonathan. "The Sources of Rasselas." New
England Quarterly, 27 (Summer 1954), 278–91.

An article in a monthly magazine:

Puttle, Gary. "Boswell's Medical History."
Harper's, Oct. 1972, pp. 42–52.

An article in a weekly magazine:

Uncles, Norman. "Mr. Boswell and Dr. Johnson."
Saturday Review, 26 July 1969, pp. 20–25.

An unsigned article in a weekly magazine:

"New Dirt on Boswell." Time, 4 July 1969, pp.
32–33.

Articles in newspapers:

Kirsh, Robert. "New Material on Boswell." The
Los Angeles Times, 9 Nov. 1974, Sec. 3, p. 26,
cols. 2–4.

"A New Boswell Scandal." The Spokesman Review
(Spokane, Wash.), 8 Jan. 1975, p. 12, col. 3.

27H SAMPLE PAGES FROM A RESEARCH PAPER

In preparing and submitting your research paper, follow your instructor's directions as to (1) the kind of folder, if any, to contain the paper; (2) the kind of paper to use and the method of typing; (3) the width of margins; (4) the kind of title page to prepare; (5) the kind of outline, if any, to prepare; (6) the location of footnotes; and (7) the method of entering charts, graphs, appendixes, and so on.

The following two sample pages of a research paper illustrate (1) the introductory paragraph of a research paper; (2) the introduction to and method of entering a short quotation; (3) the introduction to and method of entering a long (inset) quotation; and (4) the placement of footnotes at the bottom of a page.

SAMPLE RESEARCH PAPER

EDUCATIONAL REFORM IN SOVIET RUSSIA IN 1968

The communist leaders of the Soviet Union have always maintained that among their greatest achievements is the constitutional right of the Soviet citizens to free public education. The right to ten years of education has always existed in Soviet Russia, but the country's educational system has undergone many revisions over the decades. A close inquiry into the causes of these revisions sheds much light on the progress of the communist experiment. One American expert on Soviet education maintains that "the Soviet leaders . . . claim that they revise and update their educational system to meet the changing needs and goals of their regime, but much evidence indicates that educational changes are made chiefly for purposes of political indoctrination."[1]   It may be, according to Skolny, that it is becoming increasingly difficult for Russian youth to be indoctrinated. The extensive educational reform in Russia in 1968 seems to substantiate that conclusion.

A chief goal of Soviet education has consistently been to abolish the social and economic distinctions between manual and mental labor, and of course this goal is political and need not necessarily pertain to the quality

[1]Nicholas Skolny, <u>Education in the U.S.S.R.</u> (New York: The New Press, 1972), p. 4.

of education.[2] Thus it behooves the careful student of communism to examine closely the details of any extensive reform in the educational system. The details of the 1968 reform centered around the polytechnization of all the schools.

In order to further merge the images of manual and mental labor, the schools set about to create in Russian minds an association of productive labor with theoretical learning. After witnessing firsthand many of the educational changes begun in late 1967 and pressed vigorously in 1968, educational expert Ina Kovarsky reported that

> The intent to associate learning with productivity begins in the first grade as pupils learn that recognizing words can be useful, in getting into the right room, for example, as well as just intellectually stimulating. As soon as pupils begin to learn some general physics, their learning is associated with vocational training and not just theory. Grades that older students receive for learning theory are openly compared with their productivity in their part-time jobs. A bright student but poor producer is not praised. No method seems to be spared to erase from the students' minds any idea that intellectuality is superior to physical productivity.[3]

Kovarsky goes on to evaluate the quality of Soviet teaching and comes to some conclusions unflattering to the communists.

[2]James Boroday, "Report from Russia," New Republic, 27 June 1969, p. 32.

[3]Ina Kovarsky, Quality of Instruction in Soviet Education (New York: Ross and Schoenstein, 1970), pp. 8–9.

Index

Boldface numbers refer to rules, lightface to pages.

Added letters, misspelling and,
  16E: 152
Addresses and dates, comma
  with, **10I:** 101
Adjectivals, **1E1:** 31
Adjective clauses, **1A5:** 20;
  1D2: 29
  in mature sentence structure,
    26A: 230
  essential, nonessential, **10F:**
    96–99
Adjective-forming suffixes,
  1A3: 11
Adjective forms, misused, **4A:**
  48–51
Adjective phrases, in mature
  sentence structure, **26A:** 230
Adjectives, **1A3:** 10–12
  adverbs formed from, **1A3:** 12
  comparison of, **1A3:** 10
  coordinate, **10G:** 99
Anyway, any way, **22B:** 198
Apostrophe, **18:** 168–73
  in contractions, **18B:** 172
  in periods of time, **18A4:** 171
  in plural spellings, **18C:** 173
  in possessive constructions,
    18A: 168–72
  with sums of money,
    18A4: 171
  predicate, **1B2:** 25
Adverb clauses, **1D2:** 29
  comma with, **10H:** 100
  in mature sentence structure,
    26A: 230–31
Adverb forms, misused, **4B:**
  51–53
Adverbial prepositional phrase,
  4A: 49
Adverbials, **1E2:** 32
Adverbs, **1A4:** 12

comparison of, **1A4:** 12
conjunctive, **1A5:** 18
formed from adjectives,
  1A3: 12
modifying by, **4A:** 48–49
time, place, manner in,
  1A4: 13
Agencies, abbreviations for,
  14C1: 128
All together, altogether, **22B:** 198
Allude, refer, **22B:** 198
Already, all ready, **22B:** 198
Agreement, subject-verb, **6:**
  63–71
  see also Pronoun reference
Ambiguity, **1I:** 35
Ambiguous pronoun reference,
  24B: 217
Ampersand (&), **14C2:** 130
Ant-ance and *ent-ence* words, in
  spelling, **16F:** 153
Antecedents
  ambiguous, **24B:** 217
  implied, **24E:** 221
  of pronouns, **1A5:** 19; **24:** 216
  see also Pronoun reference
Appositives, **1F:** 33–34
  essential, nonessential, **10F:**
    96–99
  in mature sentence structure,
    26A: 229
Article, definite, indefinite, **1A1:** 5
Auxiliaries of verbs, **1A:** 16–17
Avenues and streets,
  abbreviations of, **14C2:** 130

B

Beside, besides, **22B:** 198
Bibliography
  form of, **27G:** 272–275

Bibliography *(continued)*
working, **27D:** 257
Book titles, underlined (italics),
14B1: 124
Born, borne, **8C:** 85
Brackets, use of, **11C:** 108–09
Brand names, capitalization of,
17A13: 164
Broadcasted, nonstandard form,
22B: 198
Broad reference of pronouns,
24C: 218
Burst, bust, **22B:** 198
But not, compound subject with,
6D2: 68

C

Capitalization, **17:** 160–65
of abbreviations, **17A:** 165
brand names, **17A:** 164
buildings' names, **17A:** 164
celestial bodies, **17A:** 165
days, months, holidays,
seasons, **17A:** 163
geographic locations, **17A:** 163
historical documents and
events, **17A:** 164
interjections, **17A:** 160
literary titles, **17A2:** 161
organizations, private and
governmental, **17A:** 164
outline headings, **17A:** 165
proper adjectives, **17A:** 161
proper nouns, **17A:** 161
relatives' names, **17A6:** 162
religious words and topics,
17A: 162
school courses, **17A:** 161
in titles, **17A:** 161

Card catalogue, **27C:** 251–53
cross-references, **27C:** 253
Case
possessive, of nouns, **1A1:** 5
of pronouns, **1A5:** 19–20; **5:**
55–62
see also Pronoun case forms
Celestial bodies, capitalization of,
17A15: 165
Centuries, lower-case letters for,
17B1: 166
Cite, site, **22B:** 199
Clarity, in mature sentence
structure, **26D:** 236
Clauses, **1D:** 28–31
adjective *(or relative),* **1A5:** 20;
1D2: 29; **26A:** 230
adverb, **1D2:** 29; **10H:** 100;
26A: 230–31
dependent, **1A5:** 20; **1B3:**
25–26; **1D2:** 28; **2A:** 38
independent, **1B3:** 25; **1D1:** 28
noun, **1D2:** 30; **26A:** 231
Clichés, **20D:** 186
Coherence, in mature sentence
structure, **26F:** 238
Collective nouns, **6E:** 68
Colloqulalisms, **20B:** 183
Colon, **11D:** 109–11
Comma, **10:** 92–103
with adverb clauses, **10H:** 100
in compound sentences,
10B: 93
with conjunctive adverbs,
3B: 45
with coordinate adjectives,
10G: 99
in dates and addresses,
10I: 101
in essential and nonessential
constituents, **10F:** 96–99

D 4
E 5
F 6
G 7
H 8
I 9
J 0

CORRECTION CHART

ab	improper abbreviation **(14C)**
agr	faulty subject-verb agreement **(6A-F)**
apos	omitted or misused apostrophe **(18A-C)**
cap	capital letter needed **(17A)**
cl	lack of clarity **(26D)**
coh	lack of coherence **(26F)**
com	omitted or misused comma **(10A-J)**
comp	incomplete or false comparison **(25A-C)**
CS	comma splice or run-together sentence **(3A-C)**
D	faulty diction **(20A-D; 21A-D; 22A-D)**
DM	dangling modifier **(23D)**
DN	double negative **(4C)**
frag	sentence fragment **(2A-D)**
glos	glossaries **(16G; 22B)**
hyp	omitted or misused hyphen **(19A-E)**
id	faulty idiom **(22C)**
ital	omitted or misused underlining **(14B)**
K	awkward construction
lc	lower-case letter needed **(17B)**
log	faulty logic **(26G)**
man	incorrect manuscript form **(14A)**
MM	misplaced modifier **(23E)**
mod	misused modifier **(4A-C)**